THINK. PROMPT. BUILD.

How Google's Gemini 2.5 Redefines Intelligence, Scales Creation, and Changes the Game for Everyone

Zaida T. Huffman

Table of Contents

INTRODUCTION – THE MOMENT AI

CHANGED GEARS

On a quiet day in early 2025, something seismic happened in the world of artificial intelligence—yet most people didn't hear the tremor. There were no flashy keynotes or viral product unveilings. No countdown clocks or fireworks. Just a silent drop on a Google server: Gemini 2.5 Pro Experimental.

Within hours, those who were paying attention—developers, researchers, AI enthusiasts—knew something was off. And by "off," we mean unlike anything they'd seen before.

Benchmarks started lighting up. On LMSYS Chatbot Arena, Gemini didn't just edge into first place—it obliterated the competition, leapfrogging OpenAI's GPT-4.5 and Elon Musk's Grok 3 Preview by more than 40 points, a margin so wide it rewrote the leaderboard. On Polymarket, the odds of Gemini winning the Arena surged overnight from 12.6% to 94%, while Grok plummeted from 83.5% to 4%.

Reddit exploded. HackerNews threads ignited. Users weren't just impressed—they were spooked.

"It's reasoning better than most people I know."

"It built a functioning 3D Rubik's Cube simulator—in one shot."

"I just gave it a messy HTML dump... and it extracted everything perfectly."

And just like that, the game had changed. Quietly. Permanently.

A New Kind of Intelligence

This wasn't just another incremental update. This wasn't GPT-3.5 to GPT-4. This wasn't about bigger models, longer contexts, or more refined fine-tuning. Gemini 2.5 marked the moment AI stopped mimicking intelligence and started demonstrating it.

At the core of this leap was a concept known as the thinking model.

For the first time in public view, an AI wasn't just reacting—it was reasoning before responding. Internally generating possibilities. Testing assumptions. Holding context. Then replying. It could solve math puzzles, write complex games, simulate 3D environments, interpret massive codebases, and build interactive tools with startling fluidity—all from one-line prompts.

It wasn't just what Gemini could do. It was how it did it. It felt less like using a tool and more like watching something think.

We've Entered the One-Shot Era

A developer writes:
"Create a Lego simulator in 3D using Three.js. Make it interactive."

Seconds later, the model returns a complete working HTML file—with snapping bricks, collision logic, mouse controls, and a touch of polish even human devs might overlook.

No step-by-step engineering. No follow-up correction. Just done.

This was happening across use cases: ant farms, virus simulators, torus knot animations, video game clones, Reddit clones, document analysis, and full-on site scrapers.

In this new era, prompting isn't just a command. It's the entire build process. What used to take hours or days of dev time now collapses into seconds—and sometimes, a single sentence.

Why This Book, Why Now

This book is not about AI hype. It's not about predicting the singularity, or feeding you buzzwords. This is a field guide to something real, right now: a new way to think, build, and interact with intelligent systems.

Over the coming chapters, you'll learn:
- What Gemini 2.5 Pro actually is—and how it quietly outpaced its rivals
- How "thinking models" change the rules of interaction, reasoning, and creation
- How one-shot prompting works (and how to do it well)
- Why Google's vertical stack—data, science, and hardware—gave it a near-unfair advantage
- What this means for developers, educators, creators, and the curious
- And most importantly, how to think alongside machines in this new age of intelligence

We'll walk through real examples, break down complex ideas in plain language, and give you the tools to not just understand what's happening—but use it.

This is the moment AI changed gears.
Not because it got smarter.
But because it started thinking.

Turn the page. Let's build.

CHAPTER I

GOOGLE'S MASTERSTROKE: GEMINI 2.5 PRO UNVEILED

When Google quietly released Gemini 2.5 Pro, it didn't feel like just another product update—it felt like the curtain had been pulled back on something we weren't entirely ready for. There was no flashy marketing campaign, no overhyped reveal. Just a sudden wave of results, benchmarks, and reactions that left even the most seasoned AI watchers blinking in disbelief. Within hours, it was clear this wasn't just a better chatbot. This was a shift in power, in potential, and in perception. Gemini 2.5 didn't introduce new features so much as it redefined what features should be. It wasn't just faster. It wasn't just smarter. It was different—built to reason, to hold more, to think. And unlike past breakthroughs that took time to prove themselves, this one landed fully formed.

A New Intelligence Emerges

When people talk about breakthroughs in artificial intelligence, they often expect them to come with noise—press releases, demos on stage, hashtags trending within minutes. But Gemini 2.5 Pro didn't arrive like that. It didn't need to. It landed without warning and immediately started doing things no one had seen from a public model before. The release wasn't wrapped in marketing hype. Instead, it quietly appeared inside Google's AI Studio under the label experimental, and with it, a new name began to circulate in developer communities and AI forums: Nebula.

That codename—Nebula—wasn't just a placeholder. It carried weight. A nebula, after all, is where stars are born. And in the case of Gemini 2.5 Pro, it was a fitting metaphor: this was something dense, complex, and bursting with creative potential, marking the beginning of a new phase in artificial intelligence. To those who got early access or stumbled upon it in the AI Studio interface, it didn't take long to realize they were interacting with a model that didn't just complete prompts—it seemed to understand them. It didn't just spit out words; it reasoned, processed, solved, and created. Not with brute force, but with something that felt dangerously close to intuition.

Technically, Gemini 2.5 Pro was built on the architecture introduced with the earlier Gemini 2.0 series, but what Google had done here was more than an upgrade—it was a transformation. Every part of its design had been stretched, fine-tuned, and pushed further. And the most important leap wasn't in its size or speed, but in how it thinks. That's what makes this model different. Not that it has more data. Not that it can handle a million tokens. But that somewhere inside all those floating point numbers and transformer blocks, it started to reason like a human would—or at least, like something trying very hard to.

The company was deliberate in how it framed the release. It didn't label Gemini 2.5 as a general-use update. Instead, it introduced it as a Pro Experimental model, signaling both its advanced capabilities and its still-evolving nature. But anyone who tried it quickly discovered that calling it "experimental" almost downplayed how powerful it actually was. In almost every category that mattered—math, coding, writing, reasoning, context following—Gemini 2.5 Pro was outperforming anything else available to the public. Including GPT-4.5. Including Claude 3.7 Sonnet. Including Grok 3 Preview. And not by a small margin. In some cases, it wasn't even close.

To the untrained eye, it may have seemed like just another large language model. But to those who know what these tools have struggled with in the past—maintaining logical consistency, solving complex problems without hallucinating, reasoning across multiple steps—Gemini 2.5 Pro was clearly operating on a different level. This wasn't just about being better. It was about being built differently.

The Shockwave Hits

What followed the quiet drop of Gemini 2.5 Pro was anything but quiet. Within hours, the AI world—developers, researchers, prompt engineers, and curious onlookers—was buzzing. Not just because Google had released something new, but because the results were coming in fast and loud. And they were unlike anything anyone had expected.

On the LMSYS Chatbot Arena, where large language models are blindly pitted against each other and voted on by real users in real-time, Gemini 2.5 didn't just claim the top spot—it obliterated the rankings. It jumped past OpenAI's GPT-4.5 and Elon Musk's Grok 3 Preview by a margin that felt surreal: over 40 ELO points in a single update. To put that in perspective, most model upgrades move up the leaderboard by a handful of points—single digits if they're lucky. Gemini 2.5 leapt by dozens, an unprecedented shift in a space where even a small gain means months of work.

It wasn't just LMSYS lighting up. On Polymarket, a real-money prediction market where users bet on outcomes, the odds of Gemini winning the LMSYS Arena skyrocketed overnight. In a matter of hours, sentiment flipped. Gemini jumped from 12.6% to 94%, while Grok plunged from 83.5% to just 4%. The market wasn't just reacting—it was making a statement. Something huge had happened. And people were betting real money on the fact that Gemini wasn't just good. It was dominant.

Reddit threads erupted across subreddits like r/LocalLLaMA, r/Artificial, and r/PromptEngineering. People weren't just impressed—they were shocked. Posts piled up of users trying everything they could think of: coding tests, logic puzzles, long-context comprehension tasks, creative writing prompts. Over and over, Gemini 2.5 passed, often with flying colors. Someone dropped in an obscure pattern-recognition problem—one that stumped GPT-4 and Claude—and Gemini nailed it in 15 seconds. Another user asked it to generate scalable SVG icons, something that typically trips up models due to the precision involved. Gemini delivered clean, usable results on the first try. Again and again, the responses weren't just accurate—they were impressively elegant.

The most common reaction? Not excitement. Disbelief. People kept testing it because they couldn't believe what they were seeing.

To understand just how big of a jump this was, you have to look back at where Gemini came from. Gemini 2.0, when it launched, had already shaken things up. It introduced the idea of "thinking models"—LLMs that paused and internally reasoned before responding, simulating a kind of step-by-step cognition rather than just guessing the next word. It was a conceptual leap, but one that still felt like a work in progress. It could be fast, but it wasn't always sharp. It had moments of brilliance, but just as often, moments of uncertainty. Users appreciated the direction, but many stuck with more consistent options like GPT-4 or Claude for critical tasks.

Then came Gemini Flash, a sibling model designed to prioritize speed and affordability. Flash delivered rapid responses and low costs, making it ideal for high-frequency tasks and integration into apps like T3 Chat. But it was clear that Flash sacrificed depth for speed—it could handle basic requests fast, but it wasn't built for heavy reasoning or high-stakes creative work.

Gemini 2.5 Pro changed all of that. It didn't just improve on its predecessors—it combined their strengths. It retained the deep thinking capabilities of 2.0, but refined them. It took the speed and responsiveness of Flash and brought them into a model that could also handle nuanced logic, complex instructions, long documents, and deeply structured output. It was balanced, mature, and sharp—not just a tool that responded, but a system that engaged with your input.

Where Gemini 2.0 often needed multiple tries or follow-up prompts, 2.5 Pro started hitting one-shots—completing entire apps, games, and interactive environments from a single well-crafted prompt. Where Flash could rapidly skim context but miss the point, 2.5 Pro could grasp it, reason through it, and return purposeful output—not just technically correct, but thoughtfully designed.

This wasn't a patch or a performance tweak. It was an evolution. Gemini 2.5 Pro didn't just move the goalposts. It built a new stadium.

Behind the Curtain: Accessing the Future

For a model that would go on to dominate headlines and forums, Gemini 2.5 Pro didn't arrive through the usual front doors. There was no splash screen announcement, no countdown timer, no keynote event. Instead, it appeared like a hidden level in a game—tucked quietly into Google AI Studio, labeled with two deceptively modest words: Pro Experimental.

To those already working in AI Studio, it felt almost like an Easter egg. You'd scroll through the available models and there it was: Gemini 2.5 Pro Experimental. There was no big explanation. Just a dropdown option and a few sparse lines noting its January 2025 knowledge cutoff, token capacity of up to 1 million, and the ability to enable tools like function calling, code execution, structured output, and search grounding.

The label "experimental" carried a bit of mystery—and maybe even caution—but that didn't stop people from clicking. Curiosity in the AI space spreads like wildfire, and it wasn't long before users began running tests. What they found wasn't an unstable beta or a prototype-in-progress. They found a machine that was already miles ahead of what they'd been using a week earlier.

One of the first things people noticed was the latency—or lack of it. Gemini 2.5 wasn't just smart. It was fast. Responses that might take GPT-4 or Claude several seconds—sometimes even full minutes for long-context tasks—came back from Gemini in what felt like a blink. Users described it as "blazing fast" and "alarmingly responsive," especially considering the complexity of the tasks it was handling. Some wondered whether they were actually talking to a lighter model. They weren't.

Despite being marked "experimental," Gemini 2.5 didn't exhibit the quirks or gaps typically associated with unreleased tech. There were no crashes. No timeout loops. No obvious blind spots. It ran with a confidence that made the word "experimental" feel more like branding than reality. In fact, the only limit most users encountered was a soft rate cap—but even that was hard to trigger. Many early adopters said they never hit a wall, even after dozens of consecutive prompts.

And the adoption didn't trickle in—it surged.

Developers building tools on top of Gemini began integrating it almost immediately. Communities like T3 Chat, which had already been using Gemini Flash for speed and cost-efficiency, started experimenting with 2.5 Pro behind the scenes. Some devs got early access through Google contacts and began testing it across real workloads. They reported that the rate limits were generous, the response quality consistent, and the model availability reliable enough to build on top of.

What began as cautious testing turned into rapid adoption. Within days, people were using Gemini 2.5 Pro to generate entire web apps, simulate realistic environments, parse massive codebases, and handle multimodal prompts that mixed text, visuals, and even audio.

On social media and Reddit, the tone of conversation shifted from "Is it good?" to "How is this even possible?" The demo screenshots looked surreal—code editors filled with rich outputs from one-line prompts, animated game environments that played smoothly in browsers, 3D renderings that rotated in real time, and precision logic applied to complex prompts with little to no correction needed.

It wasn't long before some users started comparing Gemini's performance to models like Claude and GPT-4—and not just in capabilities, but in cost. A million messages processed through Gemini Flash, a related but simpler model, cost around $1,200, while Claude had cost over $31,000 to handle less than half that load. While the pricing for Gemini 2.5 Pro hadn't been officially released yet—it was still marked experimental—people were already doing the math. And it looked good.

What made the response even more powerful was that none of this was driven by advertising. It was organic. Real people trying real things and getting results they hadn't expected. That kind of reaction is rare in tech—especially in a space as jaded and saturated as AI. But Gemini didn't feel like a product. It felt like a turning point.

In the span of a week, the early adopter community went from quietly testing a new model to openly declaring that Google had just won the round, maybe even the war. What started as whispers in Discord servers and niche forums had become a loud, almost universal refrain: Gemini 2.5 is different.

Untangling the Names: What "2.5 Pro Experimental" Really Means

As Gemini 2.5 Pro began sweeping through the AI ecosystem, a new kind of confusion started to spread—less about what the model could do and more about what, exactly, it was. The name alone—Gemini 2.5 Pro Experimental—sounded like a mouthful. Was it the same as Gemini Flash? Was it a replacement for Gemini 2.0 Pro? And what did "Experimental" actually mean?

To understand Gemini 2.5 Pro, you have to understand Google's evolving approach to naming its models. Where companies like OpenAI have mostly followed a clean numerical path—GPT-3, GPT-3.5, GPT-4—Google's Gemini line has splintered in a few different directions, each designed for specific use cases. And for anyone trying to navigate the landscape, that's made things slightly murky.

At the time of 2.5 Pro's release, there were three main categories of Gemini models in circulation:

1. Gemini Flash – a lightweight, fast, and inexpensive model optimized for speed and efficiency. It's great for

low-latency use cases and high-volume workloads, like chatbot integrations, but not designed for deep reasoning or creative complexity. Flash was the go-to model for many developers because of how cost-effective and quick it was—but it had its limits.

2. Gemini 2.0 Pro – a more powerful model released earlier, positioned for general use and deeper tasks. It introduced early versions of "thinking" capabilities but hadn't fully matured. While competent, it often fell just short when it came to complex logic or precision outputs.

3. Gemini 2.5 Pro Experimental – the latest and most advanced of them all, introduced without fanfare but clearly intended as Google's flagship model for high-level reasoning, deep context management, and creative generation. It took the thinking model concept from 2.0, refined it, and fused it with speed and accuracy levels that hadn't been seen before.

The "Pro" in the name signals that it's a more capable, more comprehensive model—built to handle intricate tasks across code, math, writing, analysis, and even multimodal inputs. It's not meant to be lean and fast like Flash, but it's surprisingly efficient given its complexity.

The "Experimental" label has caused the most confusion. At first glance, it implies something unfinished or unstable. But that's not how it performs. In fact, Gemini

2.5 Pro feels more polished than many officially launched models. The label is less about functionality and more about how Google is framing access—it's a public preview of what will eventually become a core offering, with the potential for fine-tuning, rate adjustments, or feature changes before it's officially branded under a simpler name.

There's also been some speculation that "Experimental" is a kind of license buffer—a way for Google to offer powerful capabilities while buying time to finalize enterprise pricing, integration pathways through Vertex AI, and long-term support commitments. But make no mistake: what's available now isn't a prototype. It's already outperforming everything else in its class.

Adding to the complexity, some users have seen the model flip between versions depending on their location or access route—occasionally defaulting back to Gemini 2.0 Pro due to regional availability, usage load, or rollout delays. This has led to mixed experiences, especially in edge cases where the wrong model was mistakenly accessed under the same name.

But for those with consistent access to Gemini 2.5 Pro Experimental, there's no ambiguity. Once you've seen it reason, once you've seen it generate complex working simulations from a one-line prompt, once you've fed it an entire messy HTML page and watched it extract, sort, and repurpose that data in seconds—there's no mistaking it for anything else.

Google may eventually streamline the branding—dropping the "Experimental" label and rolling 2.5 Pro into its broader Gemini product line—but for now, the name acts as a quiet signal: this is the version with the most capability. The one that's still under the radar to many, but already breaking through to those paying attention.

It's not just another model. It's the one with teeth.

What unfolded in those first few days wasn't a slow climb—it was a takeover. From crushing leaderboards to generating awe-inspiring demos off a single line of input, Gemini didn't ask for attention—it demanded it. This chapter captures that moment in time, where Google's move wasn't just strategic—it was surgical. A calculated leap into a future that others were still warming up to. And as we watched Gemini tear through the limits of what we thought was possible, one thing became clear: Google didn't just release a new model. They changed the game.

CHAPTER 2

INSIDE THE MODEL: WHAT IT DOES AND HOW IT WORKS

There's a moment when using Gemini 2.5 Pro where something shifts. You ask a question—not a simple one, but something layered, abstract, or deeply technical—and the response that comes back doesn't feel like it was guessed or pulled from a template. It feels like the model thought about it. It considered possibilities, tested a few in its mind, and then decided which direction to go. There's clarity, structure, and intent in the answer—and it doesn't read like a machine reciting facts. It reads like something that understands the weight of the question.

That's the core of what separates Gemini 2.5 Pro from everything that came before. It's not just responding. It's processing, reasoning, anticipating. In this chapter, we'll strip away the hype and take a closer look at what's actually happening under the hood—how the model structures its thoughts, how it navigates complexity, and what "thinking" even means in the context of artificial intelligence. Because once you understand the internal mechanics of Gemini 2.5 Pro, you stop seeing it as a chatbot—and start seeing it as a different kind of system entirely.

The Rise of Thinking Models

If you've used AI tools before—maybe GPT-3 or Claude or even earlier versions of Gemini—you're familiar with the way they respond. You type in a prompt, and it instantly generates text back, sometimes impressively accurate, sometimes way off. What most of those models were doing was predicting the next most likely word based on everything that came before. They didn't really "think." They just filled in blanks, rapidly and at scale.

Gemini 2.5 Pro changes that.

What makes it different—what's turning heads across the AI space—is that it doesn't just start talking the moment you hit enter. Instead, it thinks first. Not metaphorically. Literally. Before responding, Gemini 2.5 Pro goes through a dedicated internal process, where it generates a series of reasoning steps behind the scenes—what you might call its internal monologue.

This is what's meant when people call it a "thinking model." It means the model pauses to deliberate, simulate, and explore possible directions before finalizing its output. In many cases, it's essentially solving the problem out loud to itself, but you don't see that part—unless you're using the AI Studio interface, which briefly displays these internal tokens as they're being formed.

For example, when you ask Gemini 2.5 a logic puzzle or a coding challenge, it doesn't just leap to a final answer. It might first ask itself, "What kind of problem is this? What rules apply here? What are the different paths I could take?" That entire internal sequence is composed of tokens—the basic units of AI thinking, like syllables or word chunks—which are generated, discarded, refined, and branched until the model arrives at a confident response. Only then does it present the polished final output to you.

To be clear, these aren't thoughts in the human sense. Gemini isn't conscious. It doesn't reflect or feel or second-guess the way we do. But it does simulate reasoning in a way that previous models did not. It lays out invisible scaffolding behind every answer—structures of logic, pattern matching, and contextual analysis that help it land more precise and useful results.

This internal monologue—technically called token-based reasoning—isn't new in concept. OpenAI explored something similar in early versions of "chain-of-thought" prompting, where you could nudge a model to explain its steps before giving an answer. But Gemini doesn't need to be nudged. It does it automatically. It's part of how the model operates. And the results speak for themselves.

Users have noticed that this process makes Gemini 2.5 remarkably effective at handling tasks that require structure: math problems, multi-step logic, debugging code, following long instructions, interpreting diagrams, generating structured documents. Instead of guessing its way through or hallucinating plausible-sounding responses, Gemini maps out an internal reasoning path. That's why it often feels like the model "gets it." Because it's simulating the kind of deliberate thinking we expect from a skilled problem solver.

In AI Studio, some of this internal thinking is visible in real time. You'll see bursts of tokens appear before the actual answer starts to form—text strings that show the model weighing options or setting parameters. But if you're using Gemini through the API or other platforms, you won't see any of that. The final answer arrives, clean and complete, as if by magic. The thinking happens in the shadows, out of view.

This behind-the-scenes reasoning also comes with trade-offs. For one, it adds a small delay. Gemini 2.5 isn't always the fastest model off the line. Sometimes it pauses for a beat longer than you'd expect. But that extra second or two often leads to dramatically better results. It's like talking to someone who doesn't rush to answer, but instead pauses, considers, and then replies with clarity.

Another side effect is that Gemini can occasionally overthink. In rare cases, it gets tangled in its own reasoning, or starts solving a problem that wasn't actually asked. This is part of the growing pains of "thinking models"—they're still being refined. But even with those occasional misfires, the upside is undeniable. When the model nails it—and it does so often—it feels eerily intentional.

There's a kind of elegance to it, really. Not just the speed or accuracy, but the way Gemini 2.5 navigates complexity. It doesn't panic when the prompt is long or weird or full of nested requests. It doesn't guess when the answer isn't obvious. It just starts working through it, one token at a time, building an invisible lattice of logic beneath its reply.

For the end user, this feels like a quiet revolution. No special commands, no prompt engineering hacks. Just normal input—and a model that now thinks before it speaks.

From Guessing to Solving

What makes Gemini 2.5 Pro feel so different in use isn't just that it thinks—it's what that thinking enables. Because when you give most language models a complex problem—something that involves multiple steps, logical gates, or abstract reasoning—they often fall apart in subtle ways. They miss details. They skip steps. They give you an answer that sounds right, but doesn't hold up under scrutiny.

Gemini doesn't do that. Or at least, it does it far less often.

The reason is simple: its internal thinking process gives it more room to get things right. When Gemini receives a task, it doesn't treat it as a fill-in-the-blank exercise. It treats it like a challenge to be solved—and before it gives you anything back, it does the work internally to figure out how that solution might look.

You can see this in real-time when it handles logic problems, especially ones that involve multi-part dependencies. Where other models may try to shortcut the answer—leaping from prompt to prediction—Gemini walks the path step by step. It's not just smart. It's methodical. And that methodical approach is exactly what makes it stand out in tasks that require tight, layered reasoning.

Take something as deceptively simple as a logic puzzle involving conditionals: If A is true, and B is false, what must C be? In earlier models, or even in current ones like GPT-4 or Claude, you might get a half-baked answer—plausible, but shallow. Gemini, by contrast, pauses. It unpacks the implications. It tracks the assumptions, holds them in memory, and applies them sequentially. The result is often a clean breakdown of why the answer makes sense, not just what the answer is.

In coding, this shows up in the way Gemini handles unfamiliar frameworks or unusual tasks. Instead of assuming it knows what you want, it analyzes your prompt structure, tests out a few possible approaches internally, and then delivers a response that reflects actual understanding. You're not just getting copied code snippets—you're getting synthesized logic, shaped by reasoning, not repetition.

And then there's math, the great weakness of many LLMs. Where most models get tripped up in multi-step calculations or subtle algebraic rules, Gemini 2.5 Pro stands out. It doesn't always get every equation right, but when it does make mistakes, they're fewer, less random, and often rooted in understandable logic. It's trying to work through the problem, not just memorize the outcome of similar problems it's seen before.

This ability to reason carefully—rather than predict reactively—is what elevates Gemini above the rest. But how exactly does it compare to other top models like GPT-4 and Claude 3.7?

That's where things get especially interesting.

OpenAI's GPT-4, for instance, is still widely considered one of the most capable general-purpose models. It's fluent, creative, and highly tuned for alignment. It's excellent at sounding confident and giving answers that are usually directionally correct. But GPT-4 doesn't think in the same way Gemini does. Its outputs are often based on deep pattern matching, rather than deliberate internal reasoning. You can prompt GPT-4 to "think step by step," and sometimes that improves performance—but it doesn't inherently need to think to produce a response. It's extremely good at predicting what sounds right, which means it excels at fluency and synthesis—but it can still stumble when accuracy depends on careful internal logic.

Then there's Claude 3.7 Sonnet, Anthropic's latest. Claude is thoughtful and polite by design, with a strong focus on safety and structured output. It's often praised for being gentle in tone and precise in long-form writing. Claude also simulates a kind of internal thought process, especially when solving hard problems—but it leans heavily on instruction-following, often trying to please the user more than solve for depth. It's great with summaries, reflections, and structured analysis, but it can sometimes miss the mark when pushed into unfamiliar or abstract reasoning territory.

Gemini 2.5 Pro is different. It feels less like a helpful assistant and more like a solver. It's not always trying to phrase things nicely or follow social cues. It's trying to figure things out. The tone may be more neutral at times, but the answers are often sharper. You can feel it in the way the model navigates a complex request—not just completing tasks, but dissecting them. Whether you're asking it to generate a physics simulation, analyze thousands of tokens of code, or solve a logic gate problem, Gemini's strength comes from the fact that it's doing real reasoning underneath the hood—and that reasoning flows into the result.

This doesn't make it perfect. Like any model, it has limits. It can still hallucinate. It can still misunderstand vague prompts. But what makes Gemini special is that when it does get things right, it's not because it's lucky—it's because it thought through it. And when you experience that firsthand—when you ask a tough question and see the model reason it out right in front of you—it stops feeling like you're talking to a chatbot.

It starts feeling like you're working alongside something that knows how to think.

Why Thinking Changes Everything

The ability to think, even in a limited, tokenized sense, changes how a model performs—but more importantly, it changes what you can trust it with.

For years, one of the biggest weaknesses in AI systems has been reliability, especially when complexity increases. It's easy to make a model sound smart. What's hard is making it consistently right when the task involves nuance, edge cases, or layers of logic that can't be skipped. That's where previous models have always struggled—when the prompt wasn't clean, when there were too many moving parts, when the desired outcome wasn't obvious from the words alone.

That's also where Gemini 2.5 Pro starts to shine.

Because it reasons internally before responding, Gemini can handle ambiguity better, follow instructions more carefully, and connect dependencies more accurately. It doesn't just look for patterns—it builds them. It doesn't race to answer—it works through the puzzle. And when that kind of process is embedded deep into the model's architecture, it leads to responses that feel less brittle. Less likely to break. Less likely to go off the rails because one part of the request was slightly confusing.

This has huge implications for real-world applications, especially in fields like software development, science, data analysis, and education—where trust and precision matter more than polish. When a model can reason across multiple steps, hold variables in mind, remember constraints, and follow through to completion without jumping to conclusions, it opens the door to more autonomous systems, more complex workflows, and more reliable agents that don't constantly need babysitting or manual cleanup.

It also changes how you interact with the model. Instead of crafting your prompt like a magic spell and hoping it lands, you can write more naturally. More messily. You don't have to hold every step in your head, because the model is actually doing the mental lifting for you. That alone makes AI more usable—not just by experts, but by anyone who wants to think through problems with a capable, consistent assistant.

But there's a catch—at least for now.

The version of Gemini 2.5 Pro that people have fallen in love with—the one showing off this kind of deep internal reasoning—is only fully visible inside Google AI Studio. That's where users have been able to watch the thinking happen in real time. They've seen the model's internal monologue take shape as tokens begin to form and vanish, tested and tossed before the final answer even appears. It's in those moments that you realize just how powerful this system is—not because of what it says, but because of everything it does before it speaks.

When accessed via API, though, this layer of transparency disappears.

The same model still performs, and you still get high-quality answers, but the token-based thought process is hidden. There's no peek behind the curtain. No visibility into how it arrived at the conclusion. You just see the end result, like any other model.

This lack of visibility might not matter for casual use, but for developers, researchers, and AI builders trying to understand, debug, or refine Gemini's behavior, it's a noticeable gap. Without access to the thinking phase, it becomes harder to distinguish between a well-reasoned answer and a lucky one. And for those trying to build trustworthy AI systems, that distinction matters.

Google has acknowledged this difference, but as of now, the API version of Gemini 2.5 Pro does not expose the internal thought stream. That stream, visible only in Studio, is what makes it possible to evaluate how the model approaches a problem, where it might have gone wrong, and how it could be improved. Without it, users are left in the dark—relying on output quality alone to measure reliability.

There's hope that this will change. The demand is clear. Developers want more than just answers—they want traceability. The ability to see how a model thinks is not just a novelty—it's a requirement for responsible development in high-stakes environments. Whether it's debugging an autonomous agent, generating regulatory explanations, or just ensuring that your AI didn't hallucinate the last 200 words, visibility into the model's reasoning is essential.

Until that happens, Gemini remains partially obscured outside of AI Studio. Still powerful, still groundbreaking—but with some of its most valuable features dimmed for those using the API.

That said, the capability is clearly there. The thinking is happening. The reasoning is real. And for those who have seen it in action, it's hard to go back to anything else. Because once you've worked with a model that can truly think through complexity—not just handle it—you stop wondering whether AI can be trusted with difficult tasks.

You start wondering how long it'll take for everything else to catch up.

The more you look at how Gemini 2.5 Pro works, the more the old metaphors fall apart. This isn't a parrot predicting your next word. It's not a glorified search engine. It's not just a language model trying to impress you with fluency. It's something else—something with structure, with memory, with strategies of its own. The architecture is still based on transformers. The foundation is still data and pattern recognition. But the behavior? That's starting to resemble thought.

By the end of this chapter, it becomes clear: the future of AI won't just be about bigger models or more data. It will be about how models think. And Gemini 2.5 Pro isn't just showing us where that future is going—it's already living in it.

CHAPTER 3

THE ONE-SHOT REVOLUTION

There was a time when building anything with AI felt like a dance. You'd write a prompt, get something back, adjust it, try again, and repeat the loop—tweaking, correcting, rewriting, and hoping the model would eventually understand what you meant. Sometimes it worked. Often it didn't. You had to babysit the process. You had to engineer the prompt just right.

Then Gemini 2.5 Pro showed up and changed the rhythm entirely.

Suddenly, you could write a single sentence—just an idea—and watch it explode into a complete, working output. Not a fragment. Not a suggestion. A full simulation. A functioning app. A game with physics, controls, visuals, even nuance. All from one line. No follow-up needed.

This wasn't just a quality-of-life upgrade. It was a tectonic shift. One-shot prompting wasn't a gimmick—it became the new standard. In this chapter, we'll step into that moment where AI stopped being a back-and-forth assistant and became something closer to an instant collaborator, capable of building entire experiences from a single breath of instruction.

When One Sentence Becomes the Whole Thing

Imagine typing a single sentence—just a raw idea—and within seconds, you have a working game. Not a mockup. Not a half-baked placeholder. A full, playable experience with controls, sound effects, visuals, and logic that makes sense.

That's one-shot prompting.

At its core, one-shot prompting is the ability to give an AI model a single, well-phrased instruction and receive a fully realized, high-quality output in return. No follow-up needed. No debugging. No five-step back-and-forth to clarify your intent. It's exactly what it sounds like: one shot to build something meaningful—and Gemini 2.5 Pro nails it.

This isn't the first time people have talked about one-shot generation. It's been a dream in AI circles for years. Earlier models, including GPT-3 and GPT-4, sometimes pulled it off—but inconsistently. You had to write clever prompts, include examples, guide the tone, format your instructions just right. It was less about what you wanted and more about how well you could trick the model into understanding your meaning.

Gemini 2.5 Pro doesn't need to be tricked. It needs to be told.

You might write something like:

> "Create a 3D Lego-building simulator using Three.js. Bricks should snap together. Include camera and rotation controls. All code in one HTML file."

That's it. No additional context. No fine-tuning. No multi-part request chain. And yet—what comes back is exactly what you imagined, often with thoughtful details added that you didn't even ask for: different brick sizes, accurate textures, sound feedback when bricks connect, a snapping system that prevents overlap. It doesn't just follow instructions—it interprets intent.

That's what separates Gemini's one-shot ability from the rest. It's not simply completing your prompt. It's understanding the outcome you're aiming for and reverse-engineering the steps to build it.

This makes the model feel less like a tool and more like a creative partner—one that can go from concept to execution without needing a warm-up. And the impact is massive. For developers, it means faster prototyping. For creatives, it means new ways to experiment. For educators, it means you can design custom visualizations or simulations in seconds. And for anyone just curious about what's possible, it means you don't need technical fluency to create something real.

One-shot prompting isn't about writing the perfect line. It's about expressing an idea clearly—and watching AI run with it.

It's not a shortcut. It's a shift.

One Line, Infinite Possibilities

The internet lit up the day people started testing Gemini 2.5 Pro's one-shot ability with more than just to-do lists and travel plans. What followed was a series of jaw-dropping examples—each one proving that the model wasn't just capable of solving problems. It could build worlds, simulate behavior, and animate ideas, all from a single prompt.

One of the earliest and most widely shared examples was the Rubik's Cube visualizer. At first glance, it didn't seem revolutionary. A 3D cube? Sure, plenty of tools could do that. But what Gemini 2.5 did was different. It generated a fully functional, rotating 3D Rubik's Cube from scratch—with persistent color tracking, customizable dimensions, and the ability to scramble and solve itself. And it didn't just look right—it was right. Every rotation behaved accurately. The cube didn't just spin; it remembered where each square had moved, even through dozens of twists. Other models attempted this and fell apart—colors shifted randomly, faces misaligned, the cube broke down under pressure. Gemini solved it in one clean shot.

Next came the interactive Lego builder, a standout not just for what it did, but for how effortlessly it did it. The prompt? Simple: build a 3D Lego simulation in one HTML file using Three.js. What Gemini returned was stunning. Bricks snapped together with realistic sound and collision feedback. A grid-based system aligned connections. Users could rotate the scene, drag bricks, change colors and sizes—all without needing extra files, libraries, or dependencies. Everything lived in a single HTML file. No installation. No errors. Just drag, drop, build. For anyone who grew up with Lego, it felt like a digital dream—one assembled by AI in seconds.

But Gemini wasn't just building toys. It was reimagining them.

The Snake game was next, but this wasn't the pixelated version from a flip phone. This was a visually enhanced, evolved version of the classic. With one line of instruction, Gemini created a version with glowing trails, particle explosions, and background gradients that pulsed when food was eaten. Different types of food granted temporary power-ups—speed boosts, reversed controls, time slowdowns, and more. The snake's appearance evolved with each new level, adding biomechanical textures and color shifts. The game wasn't just playable. It was addictive. And it had flavor—something that would take most solo developers days to build from scratch.

Then came something more organic: the ant farm simulation. Modeled after childhood toys where ants dig through sand or gel in a transparent container, Gemini recreated the concept with a smooth, side-view 3D rendering. Ants tunneled through terrain, searched for food, interacted in real-time. The prompt was casual: build an interactive ant farm using 3D visuals and realistic behavior. The output? Striking. When asked to add controls, Gemini responded instantly—users could change the number of ants, the rate of digging, the type of terrain, even the time of day. And all of it worked seamlessly. It wasn't just a visual—it was a living system with emergent behavior.

But perhaps the most jaw-dropping demo was the virus/cell battlefield simulation. In this prompt, the AI was asked to create a dynamic bloodstream environment filled with red blood cells, white blood cells, and various types of viruses. That's all. No step-by-step instruction. No predefined mechanics. Just the core concept. What Gemini delivered was a fully functioning simulation with sliders for virus replication rate, immune response speed, blood flow intensity, and more. The viruses attacked. The white blood cells defended. The balance shifted based on real-time adjustments. Watching it unfold was like peering through a microscope—except the microscope had a control panel, and AI built it from scratch.

As if to prove that it could handle pure visuals too, someone prompted Gemini to build a 3D torus knot viewer. The torus knot—complex in geometry and beautiful in motion—is a test of rendering and control. Gemini didn't just render it. It added interactivity: sliders for radius, thickness, color, wireframe toggles, lighting controls, opacity, rotation speed, and ambient intensity. Users could twist the shape, change the material, animate its movement, or reduce it to skeletal form—all from a browser window, no external libraries needed.

And finally, in what started almost as a joke, someone asked Gemini to build a surgery toy simulator. Think Operation meets digital sandbox. The AI was told to create a game where a scalpel makes cuts, the patient reacts, and you can suture them up. Gemini responded with a surprisingly intuitive simulation: a digital body that opened up with clicks, feedback on precision and stability, and dynamic visual changes depending on how steady or reckless your hand was. It wasn't going to train real surgeons—but it certainly entertained and impressed.

What all these examples share isn't just the polish. It's the completeness. These weren't demos stitched together with effort. They were full outputs, generated cleanly and logically in one shot. Each one told the same story: the prompt is now the blueprint. If you can describe what you want, clearly and directly, Gemini can build it. Fully. Immediately.

It didn't just change what was possible with AI.

It changed what we expect from it.

The Art of Saying Just Enough

What surprised people the most about Gemini 2.5 Pro wasn't just what it could do—but how little it needed to do it.

All those demos—games, simulations, visualizers—they weren't created by AI researchers writing three-paragraph prompts packed with technical jargon. They were built by people writing the kinds of sentences you'd scribble in a notebook. Simple. Casual. Sometimes incomplete. And yet the model filled in the blanks like it had been part of the conversation all along.

A lot of users started by just asking directly, without overthinking:

> "Build an interactive Snake game with particle effects and power-ups using Python and Pygame."

> "Create a Lego builder with 3D visuals using Three.js. Bricks should snap into place and rotate."

> "Make a 3D virus simulation where white blood cells attack viruses in a flowing bloodstream."

That's it. No code samples. No examples. No step-by-step instructions. Just clear intent.

And what Gemini did in return was more than a best guess—it was a structured response, often complete, with interactive components, logic flows, controls, and attention to detail that most models would require two or three follow-ups to achieve. The reason this worked wasn't just because of Gemini's technical architecture. It was because the users learned how to do something most people skip over:

They trusted the model to do the heavy lifting—and gave it just enough to guide the outcome without smothering it.

So how do you actually write a one-shot prompt that lands?

It starts with understanding what Gemini 2.5 is good at. You're not just giving it keywords. You're giving it an idea with direction. The best prompts hit three marks:

1. Clarity of intent – What do you want to build or generate?
2. Form or medium – Is it a game? A simulation? A single HTML file? Python? 3D?
3. Key features or requirements – What's most important? Interactivity? Visuals? Specific logic?

Let's break that down with an example.

Bad prompt:

> "Make a cool app with JavaScript."

There's no direction. No purpose. No features. The model will try something, but the result is likely to be vague and underwhelming.

Better prompt:

> "Build a single HTML file with a 3D environment where users can move Lego bricks around and snap them together. Use Three.js. Include rotation and camera controls."

This is short—under 40 words—but packed with intent. It tells the model what to make, how to make it, what libraries to use, and what experience the user should have. That's the sweet spot.

You don't need to micromanage Gemini. You don't have to tell it how to load the libraries, or what grid size to use, or what color the bricks should be. If those things matter, add them. But often, Gemini handles the missing details intelligently because its internal reasoning fills in what a human developer would intuitively do.

Want to go a level deeper?

You can follow a format that mirrors a creative brief:

- Title: what it is (e.g., Snake Game with Power-Ups)
- Platform/Language: Python, JavaScript, HTML, etc.
- Core features: glowing trail, multiple food types, animations
- Rules or constraints: all in one file, no dependencies, responsive design

- User interactions: click to move, keys to rotate, slider for speed

You can structure that like a list or write it in plain English. Gemini doesn't care about formatting—it cares about coherence. As long as the idea flows, it will follow.

Here's a real-world style prompt that worked perfectly:

> "Write a 3D ant farm simulation with transparent plastic walls, realistic sand/gel substrate, and animated ants that dig tunnels, carry food, and interact. Use Three.js. All in a single HTML file. Add controls to change number of ants, dig speed, and food rate."

This is gold. It reads like someone describing an idea to a colleague. Not a programmer. Not an engineer. Just a person with a vision. And Gemini responds like a builder who knows exactly what tools to use.

Another trick users found useful? If your prompt feels too short or vague, you can expand it using another model—often ChatGPT or Gemini itself. You'd write the seed of the idea and ask:

> "Expand this into a more detailed prompt suitable for a one-shot code generation."

That step alone made a huge difference. The expanded version usually included features the user hadn't thought of—realistic feedback sounds, collision detection, sliders for customization—and gave Gemini enough precision to produce shockingly complete results.

The most effective prompts struck a balance: detailed enough to guide, open enough to allow creativity. Gemini doesn't need you to do its job. It just needs a destination and a few signposts. The rest, it handles on its own.

And the more users leaned into that, the more they realized that they didn't need to be engineers or coders or designers. They just needed to speak clearly.

The model would do the rest.

From Idea to Output—Without the Drag

As more users began experimenting with Gemini 2.5 Pro, a clever pattern emerged. Instead of obsessing over the perfect prompt right out of the gate, they used other AI models—especially ChatGPT—as a kind of creative booster. They'd start with a rough sentence, then ask:

> "Can you expand this into a more detailed prompt for code generation?"

And just like that, what began as a half-formed thought was reshaped into a clean, instructive brief. One that Gemini could pick up, interpret, and execute—often in a single shot.

This prompt expansion technique quickly became a go-to trick for non-developers, designers, educators, and even experienced engineers who didn't want to spend time crafting hyper-specific instructions. Instead of struggling to phrase everything perfectly, they'd outsource the structuring. Use ChatGPT to build the bones. Then let Gemini build the house.

And this isn't just a productivity hack. It's a gateway.

Because what prompt expansion unlocks—especially when paired with a one-shot-capable model like Gemini—is speed. Not marginal speed. Not "a little faster." We're talking about collapsing days of work into minutes.

In traditional workflows, even the most basic build—let's say a game prototype—might involve planning features, setting up frameworks, sourcing assets, writing code, debugging, testing. Hours if you're good. Days if you're not.

Now?

You write a sentence.

You expand it.

You paste it into Gemini.

And the result is often ready to run.

It's not just faster. It's accessible. You don't have to be technical. You don't have to understand what a shader is or how 3D rendering works. You just need an idea—and the patience to phrase it clearly. That's all. Which means that a classroom teacher can build a science simulation for students. A hobbyist can test a game mechanic without hiring a developer. A startup founder can generate a product prototype to show investors.

The bar has been lowered not in quality—but in friction. You no longer need permission to build. You just need a sentence.

This shift doesn't just save time—it reshapes where creativity begins. Because if execution is instant, the bottleneck moves upstream to imagination. The question isn't "Can you build it?" It's "What do you want to build?"

That's why one-shot prompting isn't a gimmick—it's a redefining force. Speed alone would be valuable.

Accessibility alone would be groundbreaking. But both together? That's how tools become movements.

What used to be locked behind skill, gatekeeping, or sheer technical overwhelm is now open. The interface is language. The compiler is thought. And the output isn't half-finished. It's working code, working design, working systems.

That's not just acceleration.

That's reinvention.

What once took a team of developers, designers, and countless lines of code can now begin with a few clear words. One-shot generation is more than a technical milestone—it's a redefinition of how we bring ideas into existence. Gemini 2.5 Pro doesn't just respond to prompts; it understands intent. It sees the shape of what you want and builds toward it—not with brute force, but with insight.

As the gap between imagination and execution collapses, one thing becomes clear: we're no longer iterating on outputs. We're prompting outcomes. And in this new paradigm, the only limit isn't the tool—it's the clarity of the idea behind the prompt.

Turn the sentence into a simulation. The idea into an interface. The prompt into a product. That's the power of one-shot. And we're just getting started.

CHAPTER 4

CODING WITH AI: THE NEW DEVELOPMENT WORKFLOW

There's a shift happening quietly but rapidly in the way code is written. Not just faster. Not just with shortcuts. But fundamentally different—collaborative, iterative, and increasingly driven by language rather than syntax. For decades, development meant knowing the tools, the languages, the patterns. Now, it means knowing how to talk to the model.

With Gemini 2.5 Pro, AI isn't just helping developers code—it's becoming part of the development process itself. Not a sidekick. Not a spell-checker. A thinking collaborator that can sketch, scaffold, refactor, debug, and even architect systems on command. From building agents to translating legacy codebases to rewriting entire apps into new frameworks, this chapter unpacks how the act of programming is being rewritten in real time—one prompt at a time.

When the Model Writes the First Draft

The first time you watch Gemini 2.5 Pro build a working web app from a single line of text, it doesn't feel like automation—it feels like witnessing a new kind of intelligence in motion. It's not just copying from a template. It's building with awareness, stitching together logic, structure, interactivity, and even style. For many developers, this was the moment it clicked: Gemini isn't just generating code—it's reasoning through development decisions.

Across the board, Gemini 2.5 Pro has shown significant strength in areas where traditional LLMs tend to trip: full-file generation, understanding intent, dynamic user interfaces, and most notably—agentic coding. This is a new standard in AI programming, where the model doesn't just return a block of code, but takes on the role of a collaborative agent—able to set up files, write reusable functions, edit previous outputs, and refactor its own work based on feedback.

This shift is most evident in the SweetBench results. SweetBench is an emerging benchmark used to test agentic coding capabilities—how well a model can act like a developer, handling multiple steps of a project, building in context, not just outputting single solutions. On this benchmark, Gemini 2.5 Pro scored 63.8%, a leap forward over Gemini 2.0 and competitive with the best coding models available. And that score came from a custom agent setup, proving that with the right orchestration, Gemini can perform at a level that makes it viable for real development tasks.

Where it really shines is in code transformation, editing, and creative architecture. It's particularly good at taking vague or high-level prompts—things like "Convert this Python script into a modern web app using React," or "Add animations to this canvas-based game,"—and returning results that feel almost like they were written by a junior developer who knows your intent. It's not perfect, but it often gets you 80% of the way there, and that's enough to change the pace of an entire dev workflow.

But with that said, Gemini's performance is not without limitations.

It's still not the most precise model when it comes to low-level algorithmic challenges or highly specialized framework quirks. In those areas, especially ones that involve obscure syntax, deeply nested logic, or complex backend infrastructure, it can stumble. Sometimes it hallucinates functions. Sometimes it returns solutions that feel correct but quietly fail in edge cases. And while it reasons well through structure, it occasionally gets lost when dealing with unusual APIs or new library updates that weren't included in its training data.

Another limitation—particularly for developers using the API—is the lack of visible thought process during coding. In AI Studio, Gemini often reveals its thinking path, making it easier to debug or understand why a certain approach was taken. But in API implementations, that internal reasoning is stripped away. You're left with the final output, clean but opaque. That's fine for fast prototyping, but it can make troubleshooting harder when the model gets it wrong.

Still, for the majority of coding tasks—especially front-end apps, interactive demos, and code-heavy prototypes—Gemini doesn't just hold its own. It often leads the pack.

One of the most striking examples was the generation of a full Lego-building simulation in 3D. The user asked for snapping bricks, visual feedback, and full interactivity—all in one file. Gemini delivered. Not only did it include realistic geometry and controls, it built a clean user interface, intuitive snapping logic, and even added polish like color selection and collision handling. There were no follow-up instructions. Just one prompt. And that kind of delivery is where Gemini's strengths shine brightest: full-context, goal-driven, intentional code.

And that's the real value—not just that it writes syntax, but that it writes solutions.

As SweetBench and other agentic coding tests evolve, Gemini's role as a model that can build, reason, revise, and scaffold projects from the ground up is becoming more clear. It's not just about giving you answers. It's about giving you working foundations—the kind of outputs you can build on, ship with, or hand off.

It won't replace developers. But it will absolutely amplify them. And in many cases, it'll let people who never thought of themselves as developers step into the role for the first time—with nothing more than a prompt and a problem to solve.

When Code Becomes a Playground

The true test of an AI coding model isn't in how well it can autocomplete boilerplate or mimic a known pattern. It's in whether it can take an abstract idea—something visual, interactive, with rules and edge cases—and build it from scratch without hand-holding. That's where Gemini 2.5 Pro has consistently raised eyebrows.

What stunned early users wasn't just that the model could build things—it was how quickly it built things that actually worked.

In one widely shared demo, a user asked Gemini to build a snake game, but with a twist: make it visually striking and full of features. The model delivered a version with pulsing background gradients, glowing trails, animated food effects, and dynamic power-ups. Different food items triggered mechanics like speed bursts, reverse controls, and slow motion. The snake itself evolved as it grew, with shifting textures and segmented animations. What would've taken a developer a day or two to pull off was generated in seconds—and it looked great.

In another prompt, someone requested a flight simulator. That's it. No parameters. No framework. Just "Create a simple flight sim." Gemini built a working environment where users could accelerate, pitch, yaw, and fly across a 3D-rendered landscape with shadows and lighting that mimicked altitude. Again, all from one line.

These weren't superficial mockups. They were functional, interactive, and visually coherent, ready to test or build upon. And this is where Gemini separates itself from models that can write snippets. It doesn't just write code—it creates systems.

But perhaps the most telling demo—the one that became a kind of underground benchmark for AI coding skill—was something far more specific, almost silly on the surface: the "ball-in-a-hexagon" test.

Originally proposed by a developer named Flavio, the challenge was simple: can an AI model create a physics simulation where a ball bounces accurately within a hexagon without falling out or behaving unrealistically? You'd think this would be straightforward, but it's deceptively hard. Most models struggle with geometry-based physics, particularly when collision detection is involved. The shape isn't symmetrical like a square, and the angles introduce subtle issues in bounce logic, wall detection, and friction modeling.

Models that could ace benchmarks and write clean code would consistently fail this test. The ball would pass through walls. Bounce endlessly. Slide into a corner and stick. Or worse, accelerate infinitely and fly off-screen.

Gemini? It got close. Very close.

In multiple trials, Gemini 2.5 Pro managed to generate simulations that mostly worked, with the ball staying inside the hexagon, bouncing with accurate velocity, and reacting to angles with believable physics. It wasn't flawless—sometimes the logic would break when the ball hit a corner just right—but it was leagues ahead of what earlier models could do.

Why does this matter?

Because the ball-in-a-hexagon test isn't just about physics. It's a gut-check for reasoning. It tests whether a model can internalize geometry, apply constraints, manage state, and build logic chains that hold together. It's small on the surface but huge in implications. If an AI can't manage this, how can you trust it to build a multiplayer game server? Or model a scientific system? Or simulate real-world behavior?

It became a kind of hidden benchmark in dev communities—not because it was official, but because it was honest. It exposed the model's limitations. And Gemini, unlike others, showed real signs of understanding the problem—not just regurgitating code, but attempting to solve it.

That's why these demos matter. They aren't just impressive—they're evidence. That the model isn't copying. It's constructing. That it's not guessing. It's thinking through structure, interaction, and consequence.

Whether it's building a virus simulation in a bloodstream, a Lego builder with grid snapping and drag-and-drop logic, or a simple toy surgery game that reacts to user precision—Gemini has shown again and again that when you give it a prompt, it doesn't just hear the words.

It sees the system behind them.

Where It Breaks—and Why That's Okay

For all the excitement around Gemini 2.5 Pro, it's important to recognize where the edges show. No model is flawless, and even one as capable as Gemini comes with trade-offs—especially when brought into real-world development environments.

One of the biggest friction points right now is how "thinking models" perform inside live editors—tools like Cursor, Replit, or even custom IDE integrations. At first glance, it seems like a perfect fit: an AI that can reason step-by-step should be ideal for assisting inside a dev environment, right?

But that's where the seams start to stretch.

The problem is timing. Gemini's ability to think—its strength in planning, simulating, and refining before it answers—comes with a slight pause. And in an editor where speed is the name of the game, that pause can feel like a drag. You ask it to refactor a function or complete a scaffold, and it takes a few seconds longer than expected.

Not much—but just enough to disrupt the flow of a fast-moving developer.

Worse, in some cases, that internal thinking becomes a liability. The model starts trying to anticipate things you didn't ask for. It gets caught in loops. It "imagines" problems that aren't there. In one notable case, when tasked with a simple gravity-based ball simulation, Gemini's internal reasoning drifted so far that it reversed gravity—launching the ball upward instead of letting it fall. Why? Because the model overthought the prompt. It invented context that didn't exist. It hallucinated intent.

This tendency to over-assume is something we've seen in other thinking models too—especially when the user is vague or when the task could be interpreted in multiple ways. Claude sometimes suffers from this. GPT-4, when asked to "think step-by-step," can occasionally overcomplicate an otherwise simple answer. Gemini's version of this quirk is subtle but real. It's not that the model is wrong—it's that it's too eager to be clever.

These moments don't happen often. But when they do—especially in the middle of live coding—they remind you that AI isn't a developer. It's a reasoning engine, and sometimes its reasoning drifts into unnecessary territory.

That said, there are still very clear zones where Gemini outshines other models.

When you need to generate complete, structured, context-aware code, Gemini leads. It understands the big picture better than almost any other public model. Give it a one-liner to build an interactive app or simulation, and it won't just return a code block—it'll create something that's wired together thoughtfully, with a front-end, behavior logic, and visual output. It gets systems. Not just code.

It's also exceptional in multi-modal prompting. If you feed it a long chunk of HTML and ask for a JS script to extract links, it doesn't choke. It parses. It processes. It builds a working solution—even when the HTML is messy or malformed. Most models struggle with messy input. Gemini doesn't flinch.

And then there's the million-token context window. If you're working with huge files—massive codebases, long documentation, sprawling API specs—Gemini holds context better than almost anything else on the market. It doesn't just remember what was said five prompts ago. It remembers what was said fifty thousand tokens ago. And that kind of memory changes how you write, build, and debug at scale.

But where Gemini still trails?

Low-level code precision. If you're building deeply optimized, high-performance systems—like a C++ rendering engine or complex data structures—it might hallucinate syntax. It might confuse library versions. Claude 3.7 and GPT-4 often edge it out on granular correctness, especially in edge-case logic or when integrating obscure dependencies.

And again, in real-time use, the latency from token-based thinking can slow down rapid prototyping. That's where Gemini Flash is better—it trades deep reasoning for speed, and sometimes that's the right call.

So what's the takeaway?

Gemini 2.5 Pro isn't perfect. It won't replace a seasoned engineer. But it changes the game by making code more accessible, more complete, and more contextual than ever before.

It's not just an assistant—it's a second mind. One that thinks in tokens, reasons in layers, and, every now and then, gets a little too creative for its own good.

And honestly? That's part of what makes it so powerful.

What's Coming Next: The Future Already in Motion

If Gemini 2.5 Pro feels like a leap, that's because it is. But according to Google, it's not even the final form. It's a checkpoint—an early access pass into something even more ambitious. And they've been surprisingly transparent about what's next.

One of the biggest changes on the horizon is the jump from 1 million to 2 million tokens of context. That's not just a bigger number—it's a transformation of what AI can hold in its mind at once. With that kind of memory, a model could ingest the entire documentation of a codebase, track all the dependencies, follow long user conversations, and still have room left over to reason deeply about each part. For devs working with sprawling legacy systems or complex product ecosystems, that's a game-changer. It means less chunking. Less summarizing. Less managing what the model can and can't remember. It means everything fits.

Google's also made it clear that the thinking model architecture isn't going away—it's the foundation of where they're headed. Future versions of Gemini will continue to lean into structured reasoning, token-based deliberation, and agentic workflows. This means more models will think before they speak, not just output the most likely next word.

There's also talk of integrated multimodality becoming default, not just a feature. Right now, Gemini can handle images, audio, code, and text within a single prompt, but soon, that kind of mixed input will be expected—and even necessary. Think uploading a PDF, describing a bug in natural language, referencing a design sketch, and getting a fully styled, functional app in return. That's not sci-fi. That's where this is going.

Internally, Google's been exploring agent orchestration, where Gemini doesn't just write code—it coordinates chains of logic, subtasks, and tool use, like calling APIs or writing files, without needing to be told exactly how. Early glimpses of this are already showing up in evaluations like SweetBench, but there's a bigger vision behind it: making AI not just a builder, but a coordinator. Something that understands not only how to write code, but when to delegate, when to wait, and how to adapt across tasks.

The company has also teased a more robust public API experience, where the full "thinking output" currently visible in AI Studio might one day be exposed in API integrations as well. That's a big deal for developers who want transparency, trust, and traceability—who need to see not just what the model decided, but how it got there. The more that reasoning becomes part of the standard interface, the more usable and accountable these systems become.

There's even speculation—backed by comments from Google's AI leadership—that Gemini will eventually be paired with native memory, allowing models to persist learning across sessions, remember previous user interactions, and evolve over time. That's where things move from "smart assistant" to something more agent-like, more autonomous. Imagine a model that not only helps you build an app—but remembers how you like to structure your components, how you prefer to write documentation, or what your design patterns tend to be. That's personalization on another level.

Of course, none of this comes without tension. The more powerful Gemini becomes, the more pressure Google will face to get everything right—rate limits, privacy, API parity, pricing. And while 2.5 Pro is still labeled "experimental," its real-world performance suggests that this is less a beta and more of a quiet rollout of the future.

For now, developers, creators, and early adopters are building with it, testing its edges, pushing it further with every prompt. But even as it reshapes the present, Gemini is clearly designed with tomorrow in mind.

And if this is just the start?

The future's already writing itself—one line of code at a time.

We're no longer just coding with AI. We're coding through it.

The lines are blurring between writing a spec and writing the code itself. What used to take hours of boilerplate now takes minutes of clear communication. And what once required entire teams can often begin with a single person, a single idea, and the right prompt.

This isn't the end of software development. It's the beginning of something more powerful: a future where technical creation is driven by logic and language, working side by side. Gemini doesn't replace the developer. It expands what a developer can do—and who gets to become one.

CHAPTER 5

INTELLIGENCE AT SCALE: THE MILLION

TOKEN WINDOW

There's a threshold in AI that most people don't think about until they hit it: context. Not intelligence. Not creativity. Just the model's ability to remember what's already been said. In earlier systems, it was the hidden bottleneck. You could only fit so much into a prompt before things started falling apart—code got cut off, instructions were forgotten, logic chains were broken. It wasn't a question of capability. It was capacity.

Then came Gemini 2.5 Pro, with something that shifted the ceiling entirely: a million-token context window.

That number changes everything—not because it sounds big, but because of what it makes possible. In this chapter, we'll explore what happens when memory expands, and how Gemini's ability to process massive input doesn't just improve output—it redefines the very structure of how we work, think, and build alongside AI.

Memory That Matters: What a Token Really Is

To understand why Gemini's million-token window matters, you first have to understand what a token actually is. Not the hype-term. The real, working definition behind the scenes.

In the simplest terms, a token is a piece of language—not quite a full word, not quite a single letter. It could be a whole word like "hello," or it could be a chunk of one, like "tion" at the end of "station." On average, a token is about four characters long. That means a sentence like "Build me a 3D weather simulator" might contain 8 to 10 tokens, depending on how it's broken down.

When you interact with a large language model, every token counts. The words in your prompt? Tokens. The model's internal reasoning? Tokens. The response? Also tokens. And there's a limit to how many can be processed at once—what's called the context window. If the conversation gets too long or the input gets too complex, the model has to forget the earlier parts. That's where things start to fall apart. Logic drops. Instructions fade. Answers lose accuracy.

For years, this context limit was the hidden ceiling of AI. GPT-3 had a cap of around 4,000 tokens. GPT-4 extended that to 8K and eventually 32K, which opened the door to longer documents and slightly more complex coding workflows. Claude 2.1 upped the ante to 100,000 tokens and stunned the community. And then came Gemini 2.5 Pro.

One million tokens.

To put that in perspective, you could feed Gemini the entire codebase of a modern SaaS platform—every file, every module, every readme—and it would still have room to reason about your next request without forgetting what came before. You could drop in a 400-page legal document, a full product manual, or a whole semester's worth of textbook material. Gemini could read it all, index it internally, and then use that as context when answering your question.

It doesn't summarize. It holds it in working memory. That's the key.

The power of the million-token window isn't just that Gemini can consume large inputs. It's that it can do something with them—reason across them, reference them directly, generate with precision based on the entire scope of what you gave it. Not summaries. Not impressions. The full content, token by token.

This alone redefines what's possible. You're no longer working with a forgetful assistant. You're working with a model that remembers at scale.

And it's only going further.

Google has already confirmed that a 2 million token window is on the way. That's not marketing—it's infrastructure. At 2 million tokens, the model could ingest and reason through entire repositories, product knowledge bases, legal frameworks, multi-document research corpora—all at once, without losing track of where anything came from.

For developers, that means you can paste your entire stack into a session and ask for real, architectural feedback. For lawyers, it means feeding in precedent and clauses across hundreds of pages. For educators, it means generating personalized material from a full curriculum. And for startups, it means creating agents that actually understand the full context of your data without piecemealing it into bite-sized chunks.

Most people don't think about tokens. But tokens are the real constraint. They define what a model can hold in its head, how deeply it can reason, and how connected its answers feel to the problem it's solving.

Gemini isn't just more intelligent. It's more present. It doesn't forget your question halfway through. It doesn't drop the thread. It holds it all—thoughtfully, deliberately, and at a scale that redefines the conversation.

This is where AI moves from a tool... to a partner.

What Becomes Possible When AI Can Remember Everything

Before the million-token window, working with AI meant working in pieces. You couldn't feed it too much at once. You had to split your documents, break your code into chunks, summarize articles, strip out irrelevant formatting—anything to squeeze your task into the limited memory of the model. And when that context ran out, so did the coherence.

But now, with Gemini 2.5 Pro, that bottleneck is gone. And what that unlocks is bigger than just convenience—it's an entirely new category of use cases that weren't even feasible before.

Take full codebase analysis, for example. One user ran Gemini through the entire T3 Chat repository—a sprawling, 200,000+ line codebase with TypeScript, backend engines, UI components, and legacy logic woven together. Normally, getting a handle on something like that takes days, maybe weeks, even for seasoned devs. With Gemini, it took minutes.

The process was simple. Clone the repo, load it into the AI, and ask natural-language questions like:

> "Where is the local storage handled for the client-side sync?"

> "What's the difference between Zero Storage and Replicache in this codebase?"

And it answered—accurately, contextually, and fast. No setup. No additional tooling. It parsed through file dependencies, inferred relationships, and returned not just the lines of code involved, but explanations of how they connected. This is what it means when we say AI can "understand code." Not just syntax, but structure. Intent. Architecture.

Another clear win is in large document parsing. Think research papers, product manuals, onboarding handbooks, or technical documentation. Before Gemini, you'd have to break a document into sections and process each chunk separately, hoping the model wouldn't lose the thread. Now? You can dump the entire thing—hundreds of pages—and just ask questions like:

> "What's the main difference between Method A and Method B in this paper?"

> "Summarize every mention of user access roles across the security guide."

No pre-processing. No manual highlighting. Just straight answers, drawn from everything at once.

It gets even more powerful when you're dealing with HTML and JavaScript scraping from massive, messy web pages. One user fed Gemini a full blog's source code—71,000 tokens of chaotic embeds, outdated tags, inline scripts, and div soup—and asked for a script to extract every YouTube and SoundCloud link from the iframes. Not only did Gemini do it, it wrote a JavaScript snippet that could be dropped directly into the console and run instantly, producing clean, copyable output.

The kicker? It figured out the expected result without being asked. It understood the goal.

That's the difference between a big context window and real comprehension. Gemini didn't just process the input—it reasoned through the structure, inferred the pattern, and returned an intelligent solution.

And then there's PDF analysis. Historically, PDFs have been a pain point for AI. They're inconsistent, often include mixed media, and wrap text around columns, images, charts, and tables that don't always translate cleanly. But Gemini, with its multi-modal awareness and massive context, treats PDFs differently. Feed it a full technical report with embedded graphs, mathematical notation, inline images, and long footnotes, and you can ask things like:

> "Interpret the trend in Figure 4 over the last five years."

> "Compare the data tables on pages 17 and 33 and explain the difference in methodology."

It doesn't blink. It doesn't lose the reference. It scrolls through the full document internally, tracks your question across pages, charts, and context—and delivers answers that actually make sense.

For educators, this means building interactive lessons from full textbooks. For scientists, it means working across full reports without reducing everything to summaries. For analysts, it means tracking insights across hundreds of pages of raw data and visuals.

What's happening here isn't just speed. It's scale with integrity. Gemini isn't just faster or better—it's deeper. It holds more, understands more, and connects the dots that other models drop when their memory runs out.

And most importantly, it means you no longer have to simplify your problem to fit inside the model.

Now the model can handle the full problem.

How It Holds So Much Without Breaking

When people hear "one million tokens," the first question they often ask is, How is that even possible? It's not just a bigger number—it's a massive technical challenge. Large context windows come with serious trade-offs in speed, cost, memory, and model performance. Yet Gemini 2.5 Pro manages to handle it—smoothly, efficiently, and without choking on complexity. The way it does that comes down to how context is managed under the hood.

To start, a language model doesn't read your entire prompt like a human would—from beginning to end, all at once. Instead, it processes everything as tokens, and the way those tokens are stored and referenced affects how much the model can "remember" and reason about at any given time. The model's attention mechanism—a core part of how it decides which tokens to focus on—has historically been quadratic in cost. This means that if you double the number of tokens, the amount of computation needed to process them goes up by four times. Multiply that out, and you can see why earlier models struggled beyond 8K or 32K tokens.

But Gemini 2.5 Pro—backed by Google's custom TPUs and architectural refinements—has clearly implemented something more scalable. While Google hasn't released full technical whitepapers (yet), users and researchers speculate that Gemini uses some combination of:

- Efficient attention mechanisms, such as sparse attention or local-global attention patterns, which reduce the cost of processing long sequences.
- Segmented memory models, allowing the model to separate long-term and short-term context, prioritizing critical tokens without overloading computation.
- Context compression, where redundant or low-value tokens are deprioritized or summarized internally, letting the model stay focused on the parts that matter most.
- Intelligent caching, especially in scenarios like code analysis or document parsing, where similar token structures repeat and can be processed more efficiently.

This allows Gemini to "see" a huge input window without collapsing under its own weight. And it's not just about holding data—it's about doing something meaningful with it. The model can reason across long documents, maintain logical flow over massive inputs, and link concepts from early tokens to late ones without forgetting or looping.

But here's what's just as important: despite the huge window, latency remains low. In AI Studio, users report that Gemini can process long prompts and still return answers in seconds, not minutes. That speaks to Google's investment not just in the model, but in the infrastructure behind it—the TPUs, the distributed systems, the optimizations that allow these massive workloads to run smoothly.

For developers, this means you don't have to compromise. You can give the model everything it needs—code, docs, user behavior logs, system specs—and trust that it won't just digest it. It'll process it efficiently, and then respond with coherence.

This also explains why Gemini feels so different in complex workflows. It's not just smarter. It's structurally more aware. It remembers across the full length of your input, and still has room to reason deeply when it comes time to generate output. You're not fighting the model's memory anymore. You're working within it.

In short, Gemini's context handling isn't just big—it's intelligent at scale. And it marks a turning point in how language models will be built and deployed going forward. No more splitting up ideas. No more rewriting prompts to fit a character limit. With Gemini, you say what you need to say, and it remembers the rest.

A million tokens isn't just about scale—it's about freedom.

The freedom to feed a model your full codebase, your entire knowledge base, your most complex, messy, nonlinear instructions—and still get a response that makes sense. It turns AI from something you query into something you can work with, at depth, without compromise.

And the ripple effects are just starting. As Gemini moves toward two million tokens and beyond, we're entering a future where memory is no longer the constraint. Context is no longer the weakness. And the only real limit left... is how much we're willing to put on the table.

Because Gemini won't just take it in.

It will remember. And it will reason with all of it.

CHAPTER 6

GOOGLE'S AI ADVANTAGE: WHY THEY' RE PULLING AHEAD

For years, Google felt like it was holding back. Despite pioneering the transformer architecture that launched the generative AI boom, it watched from the sidelines while others took center stage—OpenAI with GPT, Anthropic with Claude, even smaller players with lean, fast open-source models. But with Gemini 2.5 Pro, that dynamic flipped almost overnight. Google didn't just catch up—it started pulling ahead.

What changed wasn't just the model. It was the entire stack: data, compute, research, infrastructure, and integration. In this chapter, we unpack the full scope of Google's advantage—why they're able to move faster, scale bigger, and ship smarter than almost anyone else in the race. Because behind Gemini isn't just a model. There's a machine.

The Trifecta That Changes Everything

Ask anyone in the AI space what it takes to build a world-class model, and you'll hear the same three ingredients every time: data, science, and hardware. You can't skip any of them. You can't fake your way through. And Google, almost quietly, has built world-class dominance in all three.

Let's start with data. No company on Earth has access to a broader, richer, and more diverse dataset than Google. Decades of crawling, indexing, serving, and interpreting the internet—through Search, Gmail, YouTube, Maps, Docs, Android, and Chrome—has given Google a staggering trove of high-quality, high-context information. Not just public content, but behavioral data, structured signals, and deep taxonomies of how people actually interact with information across formats.

That matters. Because language models are only as good as what they're trained on. If your training data is narrow, noisy, or outdated, your model will hallucinate more, break under edge cases, or fail to generalize. Gemini, on the other hand, was trained with multi-modal breadth and global depth, which helps explain why it's so capable across tasks—from parsing PDFs to reasoning over spreadsheets to simulating dynamic physics.

Then there's science. This is where Google's legacy in AI really kicks in. They invented the transformer architecture—the foundation of every modern LLM. They've published breakthroughs in everything from reinforcement learning to multimodal training to retrieval-augmented generation. When you dig into AI's history, you'll find that many of the core ideas powering today's frontier models were born in Google Research.

But until recently, that scientific firepower was siloed. Models like BERT, T5, and PaLM never had the product integration or momentum of GPT-3 or Claude. Gemini changes that. It's not just research. It's research shipped.

And then there's the big one: hardware.

While most companies in the space rely on NVIDIA GPUs—high-powered, general-purpose chips that dominate AI training and inference—Google runs Gemini on its own custom TPUs (Tensor Processing Units). These aren't just faster in some abstract way. They're purpose-built for model training and inference at scale. Because Google controls both the software and the hardware stack, it can optimize Gemini to run with extreme efficiency—processing more tokens, with less latency, at a fraction of the cost.

That's not a minor edge. It's a strategic moat.

TPUs allow Google to do things others can't afford to try. Like offering a million-token context window for free. Like deploying models across billions of Android devices. Like pushing high-rate limits in AI Studio without degradation. The speed and affordability of Gemini's output isn't a miracle—it's the direct result of vertical integration between architecture, infrastructure, and deployment.

And the more they improve TPUs—and tailor Gemini's training to that environment—the wider the gap gets. Other labs might produce smarter models in isolation. But when it comes to the full picture—training, inference, reliability, cost, and scale—Google has more control, more leverage, and more raw capability than anyone else in the game.

It's easy to look at Gemini and see an impressive model.

But what you're really seeing is the outcome of years of compounding advantage—data that's unmatched, science that's baked in, and hardware that's built to win.

Owning the Stack: Where Infrastructure Becomes Leverage

One of the most overlooked parts of Google's dominance in AI isn't the model. It's the platform it runs on.

Gemini 2.5 Pro doesn't live in a vacuum. It runs natively on Google Cloud Platform (GCP), which gives Google a critical edge that most of its competitors can't replicate. Because when you control the cloud your model runs on—compute, storage, deployment, and scale—you don't just ship a model. You own the entire experience.

That matters for performance. It matters for speed. And most of all, it matters for distribution.

Right now, if you're building AI tools or agents on top of Gemini, you're doing it through Google's own AI Studio, or soon via Vertex AI on GCP. That means you're operating within the same infrastructure that powers YouTube, Gmail, and Search. It's built for global scale, real-time latency, and extreme reliability. And for developers, that translates into fewer limits, faster responses, and more room to build with serious complexity.

Compare that to OpenAI. While GPT-4 is powerful, it runs almost entirely through Azure, Microsoft's cloud platform. If you're using GPT-4 through API, you're at the mercy of a third-party cloud—one OpenAI doesn't control, but partners with. That relationship works, but it's not seamless. There are rate limits. Downtime. Uncertainty around updates. And when something breaks, the finger-pointing begins.

Anthropic's in a similar spot. Claude 3 runs on AWS, and while their model is highly capable, the infrastructure still depends on Amazon's setup. That includes pricing, rollout cadence, and deployment quirks. Their models might be sharp, but their platform control is limited.

XAI, Elon Musk's AI company, is even earlier-stage. Their Grok model is integrated into X (formerly Twitter), but outside of that ecosystem, access is sparse. There's no robust API. No broad developer tools. And critically—no real cloud. Without platform infrastructure, they're reliant on others to scale and deploy.

Then there's Deepseek—a rising player with serious momentum, particularly around open-source models. Their models are lean, fast, and increasingly impressive in benchmarks. But their Achilles' heel? Uptime. Access. Infrastructure. Developers regularly report that their API is overloaded, unstable, or flat-out unavailable. The models are good. The cloud just can't keep up.

This is where Google stands alone.

It's the only AI lab that also owns a global-scale cloud platform, a proprietary chip architecture, a search engine, a mobile OS, and an entire productivity suite—all tightly integrated. That means faster rollout, lower latency, tighter feedback loops, and full control over every part of the user experience.

You see it in AI Studio, where Gemini runs fast and smooth. You see it in the upcoming Vertex AI integration, where enterprise customers can deploy production-grade AI with granular configuration and billing. And you'll see it more as Gemini gets baked into Google Workspace, Android, and Search—because Google isn't just building a model to show off.

They're building a platform for the future of work, creation, and computation.

Everyone else has to rent the highway.

Google owns the road.

Why No One Else Can Follow the Formula

At first glance, it might seem like the AI race is neck and neck—OpenAI, Anthropic, Google, maybe a few open-source contenders catching up fast. But under the surface, the picture isn't close at all. Because while most labs are trying to optimize one part of the equation—just the model, or just the API—Google is executing across the full stack, and doing it in sync.

That's the real story here: vertical integration.

Google doesn't just build a model. It trains it on data it owns, using hardware it designs, on infrastructure it controls, and then deploys it through products that reach billions of users. Every layer of the machine feeds the next. Gemini isn't just a standalone breakthrough—it's the output of a system.

Other companies? They're still stitching things together.

OpenAI builds strong models, no question. But it has to partner with Microsoft for compute. It leases space on Azure. It's dependent on someone else's cloud to deliver the product. Even though OpenAI innovates fast, that handoff between layers slows them down when it comes to experimentation, deployment, and scale. And because Microsoft is also integrating GPT into its own products—Copilot for Word, Excel, Teams—the priorities aren't always aligned.

Anthropic faces the same challenge. Their Claude models are sharp, especially in reasoning and safety alignment, but their infrastructure story is thin. They run on AWS, rely on third-party chipsets (typically NVIDIA), and have to make pricing and performance decisions based on someone else's limitations. They can't push the boundary on context window size or token output speed without hitting scaling issues.

XAI and Deepseek are even more fragmented. One focuses on media ecosystem integration (X/Twitter), the other on open-weight performance. Both are promising. Neither has the infrastructure to roll it out at global scale—or the financial margin to keep it cheap while growing.

That fragmentation matters. Because when your chips come from one company, your cloud from another, your data from scraped public content, and your product is strapped together with API glue, you move slower. You burn more cash. You hit limits sooner. You're reactive, not proactive.

Google, by contrast, can optimize everything end-to-end:

- Data: Decades of multilingual, multi-format information across products.
- Science: Leading researchers in machine learning, vision, NLP, and more.
- Hardware: Proprietary TPUs built specifically for LLM inference and training.
- Cloud: A global network of data centers under its direct control.
- Deployment: Gemini lives inside Android, Search, Workspace, and more.

Every layer reinforces the others. Every optimization ripples through the system. That's not something you can replicate quickly—or cheaply. It's not just about talent or vision. It's about infrastructure cohesion. Google has it. Others don't.

That's why even when models from competitors catch up in raw capability, Google will still likely outpace them in speed, cost-efficiency, and scale. Because Gemini isn't running on borrowed infrastructure. It's running on a foundation built specifically for it—and for what's coming next.

When your stack is vertically integrated, you're not just shipping faster.

You're playing a completely different game.

The Charts Don't Lie: Where Gemini Leaves Everyone Else Behind

You don't have to take anyone's word for it. Just look at the numbers.

When Gemini 2.5 Pro launched, the benchmark charts told a story that felt less like a product update and more like a power shift. In the LMSYS leaderboard, where real users vote side-by-side on model output quality, Gemini didn't just climb to the top. It landed there with a record-setting margin—over 40 Elo points ahead of GPT-4.5 and Grok 3 Preview. That kind of gap doesn't happen by accident. It happens when the model is better across the board.

But it's not just about who won a benchmark. The deeper story lies in three charts that were repeatedly shown across developer reactions and early tests: price, performance, and speed.

Let's start with performance. On structured benchmarks like Humanity's Last Exam, GPQA (a science reasoning test), AIME 2025 (advanced math), and SweetBench (agentic coding), Gemini 2.5 Pro consistently took top spots—or traded blows with GPT-4.5 and Claude 3.7. But what made Gemini stand out was consistency. It didn't just excel in one area. It delivered in math, logic, coding, and long-context comprehension. That matters, because many models are specialists. Gemini is increasingly a generalist that performs exceptionally well across tasks.

Then comes speed. One of the most jaw-dropping comparisons came from side-by-side tests where developers ran coding prompts across multiple models in Cursor and VS Code. Gemini 2.5 wasn't just faster than Claude or GPT-4—it was blazingly fast, spitting out thousands of tokens in seconds, often with near-zero lag. That responsiveness isn't just a flex. It directly impacts usability. Whether you're testing ideas, generating code, or refining logic, latency kills flow. Gemini eliminates that bottleneck.

And finally—cost.

This is where things get almost unfair.

In one breakdown, a developer showed that over a million messages sent to Gemini Flash had cost just $1,200. The same volume of traffic sent to Claude? Over $31,000. That's more than 25 times the cost—for less speed, and in many cases, less performance. Even GPT-4.0, which was once considered the premium leader, now looks expensive by comparison, especially when Gemini's performance is closing the quality gap—or in many cases, surpassing it.

In another comparison chart, Gemini Flash appeared as cheap as some of the worst-performing open models, like LLaMA 3.1 or Nova Micro—but with intelligence on par with GPT-4 and Claude 3.7. That combination—cheap, fast, smart—is not something anyone else has hit yet. And it's not just a win for developers. It's a warning shot to the rest of the market.

Because if Gemini is already outperforming at these metrics while still in experimental mode, what happens when it stabilizes, prices officially drop, and models like 3.0 launch?

We're not looking at a temporary lead.

We're looking at a company with every structural advantage and a clear strategy to scale it—at enterprise, consumer, and global levels. And as these charts keep updating, one thing is becoming obvious:

Google didn't just build a great model.

They built the most cost-efficient, high-performance, large-scale AI deployment infrastructure in the world.

And they're not slowing down.

Google's lead in AI isn't accidental. It's engineered.

They have the data others can't access, the talent others try to hire, the hardware no one else can touch, and the infrastructure to roll it out at scale. More importantly, they're finally aligning all those assets—not in silos, but in synergy.

Gemini 2.5 Pro wasn't just a model update. It was Google firing on all cylinders. And if they keep this pace—across product, research, and deployment—it's not just about catching up anymore.

It's about changing the entire trajectory of what AI is, and who leads the next era of intelligence.

CHAPTER 7

REAL-WORLD IMPACT: BUILDING, LEARNING, AND PLAYING

There's a moment when technology stops being theoretical—when it moves out of labs, slides off the charts, and lands in someone's actual hands. That's where Gemini 2.5 Pro is now. No longer just an AI model breaking benchmarks or winning Reddit debates, it's quietly transforming how people build products, learn new skills, and even play.

In this chapter, we step outside the architecture and inside the lived experience—teachers building classroom tools, developers accelerating their workflows, curious users turning ideas into apps, and learners interacting with content in ways that were impossible just months ago. This is where Gemini shows its real strength—not just in what it can do, but in what it empowers others to do.

From Idea to Experience: Creators and Educators in the Driver's Seat

One of the most surprising things about Gemini 2.5 Pro is who's using it—and what they're building. Not massive dev teams. Not enterprise consultants. Everyday creators, solo builders, hobbyists, and educators are the ones putting this model to work. And they're doing it in ways that aren't just impressive—they're joyfully unexpected.

Start with the creators.

People are building games, not with weeks of coding but with a sentence or two. A single line prompt—"Build a visually rich snake game with glowing effects and animated power-ups"—yields an experience that looks like it came from a game jam submission. Not a prototype. A working, playable game with speed bursts, reverse controls, slow motion, visual trails, and polished transitions.

Another prompt results in a 3D Lego builder, where bricks snap, rotate, and click into place with satisfying feedback. No follow-ups. No tweaking. Just a simple ask—and suddenly, you're dragging colored bricks in a rendered environment with camera controls, physics, and polish you'd expect from a Unity project. But this came from Gemini. One shot.

Then there's interactive art and visualizations. Users are generating simulations of torus knots, flowing ant farms, animated viruses attacking cells, and even simple surgery games. Not only do these creations look good, they function with internal logic, user control, and UI elements—meaning they're not just visual experiments, but usable tools and toys.

The wild part? Most of these creators don't consider themselves "developers." They're designers. Tinkerers. People who had an idea and didn't want to spend hours Googling how to get started. Gemini gave them the ability to build without a background in code, and in doing so, unlocked a whole new kind of maker culture—where play and creativity are the starting point, not technical skill.

Educators, too, are leaning into Gemini in smart, quietly revolutionary ways.

Teachers are asking Gemini to create interactive science models, like ant colonies with digging behaviors, or virus-cell simulations where students can adjust replication rates and white blood cell responses. These aren't just visual aids. They're live, manipulable environments that help students understand biology in a tactile way. You can watch how systems change as variables shift, which makes abstract ideas instantly more concrete.

Others are generating math puzzles, coding exercises, and interactive quizzes that adapt based on student input. A few even use Gemini to turn full textbooks into dynamic teaching companions—asking for summaries, analogies, or lesson plans based on the text. Because of the million-token context window, entire curricula can be loaded in and referenced without needing to chunk or simplify.

What's happening here isn't flashy. It's practical. Grounded. Useful. But it's empowering in a deeply personal way. Teachers aren't waiting for official software updates. They're building their own tools, on the fly, using the language they already speak. Creators aren't stuck in tutorials. They're prompting their way through the build process.

Gemini isn't just lowering the barrier to entry.

It's removing it entirely.

And the result isn't just productivity. It's ownership.

People aren't just watching what AI can do anymore.

They're using it to do what they've always wanted to build—and never had the tools to try.

Learning Reinvented: From Static Content to Living Knowledge

For years, education technology moved at a cautious pace. Digital flashcards, self-paced video courses, PDFs with checkboxes—it was functional, but it wasn't dynamic. Now, that's changing fast. Thanks in part to tools like Gemini 2.5 Pro and the platforms building on top of it, we're seeing a shift toward interactive, AI-driven learning environments that adapt, respond, and even teach.

One of the best examples of this trend is Manis AI, a platform that's embraced what it calls "Education 2.0." It's more than a catchphrase. It's a real pivot—from passive content delivery to immersive, personalized education, powered by the kind of generative intelligence Gemini enables.

Let's say you want to learn how to build an API with FastAPI. In the old model, you'd find a YouTube video, maybe read some docs, then try it out yourself. With Manis AI, the process is different. You give it your topic, and in seconds it generates a full course module, complete with explanation, code samples, hands-on tasks, and follow-up questions. It doesn't just hand you information. It builds a learning experience, on demand.

That's a big leap. But it gets better.

One of the most popular features is automated flashcard generation, especially for platforms like Anki, the go-to tool for spaced repetition learning. Traditionally, Anki cards had to be built manually—copy-pasting definitions, questions, and answers into fields one by one. Now, with Gemini in the mix, users can feed in a textbook, a lecture transcript, or a batch of notes, and have Gemini extract the core facts, concepts, and connections—then output a polished .apkg file ready for Anki.

In minutes, you've turned a dense chapter into a spaced repetition system personalized to your learning pace.

That's not just a productivity win. It's memory engineering, simplified.

The same goes for immersive tutorials. Students and self-learners are asking Gemini to build them interactive learning tools—like a live Python sandbox that explains what each line of code does, or a physics visualizer that simulates gravity, velocity, and mass in real time. Some go even further, generating choose-your-own-path coding exercises, where Gemini adapts the next step based on how the learner did in the last one.

What used to take a full team of instructional designers and developers can now be built by one person—with one prompt.

And the reason it works isn't magic. It's context, structure, and reasoning. Gemini doesn't just output surface-level content. It understands the shape of a lesson. The flow of a concept. The importance of examples and analogies. It builds for clarity, not just completion.

This is the heart of Education 2.0: content that isn't fixed, but responds. Tools that don't just test knowledge, but help shape it. Learning that doesn't rely on memorization, but encourages exploration.

Whether it's flashcards, coding courses, or hands-on simulations, what we're seeing is the rise of AI as an educational architect—designing materials, personalizing paths, and turning static content into dynamic, evolving learning environments.

For students, it means getting exactly what they need, exactly when they need it.

For teachers, it means building smarter, faster, and at scale—without sacrificing quality.

And for platforms like Manis AI?

It means leading a wave that's not just digitizing education.

It's redefining how knowledge is built and shared.

Where Learning Looks Like Play—and Play Looks Like Creation

Not every breakthrough with Gemini 2.5 Pro is happening in classrooms or startups. Some of the most exciting use cases are happening on bedroom laptops, dorm room desks, or weekend coding sessions—where the goals aren't tied to exams or revenue, but to pure exploration.

Students are beginning to use Gemini not just as a tutor, but as a simulator—a tool to model the world, test ideas, and learn by interacting instead of memorizing. One student builds a 3D bloodstream where viruses attack cells and white blood cells respond dynamically. Another creates a physics-based ant farm where they can tweak dig speed, food drop rate, and daylight cycles. These aren't textbook problems. They're living systems that make abstract concepts real.

Instead of passively absorbing knowledge, learners are building the environments they study inside. That kind of active engagement changes everything. The model doesn't just help answer questions. It lets users ask better questions, because they can see what happens when they tweak the variables, alter the environment, or introduce new rules.

And in the same space—often overlapping with those students—is a new wave of coders doing something different entirely: they're not building apps.

They're vibe coding.

The term started as a joke in dev circles—referring to the act of coding not for function or production, but for the experience. For the aesthetic. For the feel of making something that moves, reacts, glows, pulses. A snake that leaves trails. A torus knot that shifts color in rhythm with sliders. A simulation that doesn't serve a business goal but scratches an itch in your brain.

Gemini 2.5 has become the perfect co-pilot for that kind of creative play.

Because it doesn't push back. It doesn't ask you for specs or structure. You just say, "Make a glowing ant tunnel that pulses to lo-fi music," and it builds something close enough to feel like magic. You don't worry about frameworks. You don't debug for hours. You just build. Adjust. Prompt again. Iterate. Play.

This is how a new generation is learning to code—not through lectures or textbooks, but through emotionally satisfying trial and error, where the process feels more like painting than compiling. Where the model becomes a sketchpad for interactive ideas.

The stakes are low. The creativity is high. And the learning is real.

For a student, this might mean walking away with a deeper understanding of systems thinking or conditional logic. For a hobbyist, it might mean finishing something for the first time. For a burned-out developer, it might mean remembering why they started coding in the first place.

Vibe coding isn't just a trend. It's a signal. That the tools are finally fun again. That the friction is dropping. That creation has become accessible, expressive, and immediate.

Gemini's impact isn't limited to productivity or education.

Sometimes, its most powerful contribution is that it makes building feel like play—and learning feel like freedom.

What we're seeing now isn't just AI adoption. It's creative absorption. Gemini 2.5 Pro isn't a novelty. It's becoming a tool people use daily—sometimes without even realizing how advanced it is under the hood.

From classrooms to startups, hobby projects to professional prototypes, it's reshaping how things get made. And the gap between idea and execution? It's disappearing.

This chapter is proof: when AI becomes real, it doesn't just impress.

It unlocks.

CHAPTER 8

HOW TO THINK WITH AI: PROMPTCRAFT AND

MENTAL MODELS

The biggest unlock in AI isn't the model. It's how you use it. What separates a mediocre output from a breakthrough one often comes down to a single thing: the prompt.

But prompting isn't just about typing better instructions. It's about learning to think alongside the AI, shaping your questions with intention, and building mental models for how the system reasons. This chapter explores the emerging art and discipline of promptcraft—a skillset that blends communication, logic, and creativity—and how it's redefining how we interact with machines.

Because using AI well isn't about being technical. It's about being clear, curious, and deliberate.

Prompting Is the New Interface

For decades, we've been taught to adapt ourselves to the machine. We learned the syntax. We clicked through menus. We followed structured flows built by someone else. But with models like Gemini 2.5 Pro, that dynamic flips. You don't have to speak the machine's language anymore. Now it speaks yours.

And that changes everything.

Prompting—once seen as just a way to "ask AI questions"—is quickly becoming a new creative language. It's the connective tissue between imagination and execution. A bridge between messy ideas and working outcomes. What used to require a product spec, a dev sprint, and two weeks of meetings can now start with a line like:

> "Build a responsive 3D simulation where ants dig tunnels and carry food, with camera controls and adjustable time-of-day settings."

And it just works.

But the people getting the best results aren't just lucky. They're learning the structure of this new language. They understand how to frame a prompt not just to be understood, but to guide the model's internal thinking.

They're not just typing what they want. They're shaping how the model approaches the task.

This is where prompting becomes a craft.

A great prompt isn't necessarily long. It's not stuffed with keywords. It's structured, intentional, and layered with the right signals to activate the model's strengths.

Here's a simple mental framework that many power users follow—consciously or not—when crafting a strong prompt:

1. Role / Context
    Set the tone. Let the model know what it is, or what kind of output you expect.
    "You are an expert game developer creating a playable prototype for a beginner audience."

2. Goal / Outcome
    Make the request clear, with a defined objective.
    "Build a simple 2D snake game using Pygame."

3. Constraints / Boundaries
    Provide scope, limits, or features to avoid vague output.
    "The game should include a glowing trail, speed boost power-ups, and a color-shifting background."

4. Format / Delivery Expectations

Tell it how to give you the result—code, bullet points, explanation, file-ready.

"Output the full code in a single file with comments for each section."

5. Style / Voice (Optional)

If you want the result to reflect a tone—playful, academic, concise, etc.—say so.

"Keep the game visuals fun and retro-inspired."

This structure doesn't need to be followed rigidly. But when it's applied intuitively, it gives the model everything it needs to do its best work. You're not overexplaining. You're giving direction.

And what makes prompting unique is that it's both precision and play. The best prompters are also curious tinkerers. They don't always know exactly what they're going to get—but they know how to guide the model toward something better with each iteration.

They use prompts like sketches.

And the model becomes a creative partner that paints in code, content, visuals, or logic—based on how well you frame your vision.

Prompting isn't just a workaround. It's not a stopgap.

It's a new kind of interface. And learning to use it fluently is the first step toward mastering what it really means to work with AI.

From One-Liner to Blueprint: How to Build Better Prompts

One of the most surprising revelations when using Gemini 2.5 Pro is how much it can do with so little. The one-liner prompt is no myth. People really are creating games, full web apps, simulations, and data tools with a single, casual request.

But behind every impressive one-liner is often a more refined version—an expanded prompt that brings clarity, control, and creativity to the process.

The best way to think about this is through prompt evolution. You start small, see what comes out, and then guide the model toward something more polished—not by rewriting the whole prompt, but by iterating on what you say and how you say it.

Prompt Template: Game Creation

One-liner:

> "Make a glowing snake game with power-ups and visual effects."

Expanded version:
> "Create a Python game using Pygame that replicates the classic Snake game. Add visual enhancements like a glowing trail and a pulsing background. Include various power-ups such as speed boosts, reverse controls, and temporary invisibility. Add particle effects when food is consumed, and animate the snake as it grows. Output the complete code in a single file with comments."

Prompt Template: Web App

One-liner:
> "Build a to-do list app with dark mode."

Expanded version:
> "Create a responsive to-do list web application using HTML, CSS, and JavaScript. Features should include dark mode toggle, task prioritization (low, medium, high), local storage persistence, and the ability to mark tasks as complete. Use modern UI principles and include basic styling. Output the code in a single file, ready to run in a browser."

Prompt Template: 3D Visualization

One-liner:

> "Show a 3D torus knot using Three.js."

Expanded version:
> "Create a single HTML file that renders an interactive 3D torus knot using Three.js. Include GUI controls to modify radius, tube thickness, color, rotation speed, and toggle wireframe mode. Implement camera controls, subtle lighting, and shininess adjustments for a polished look. Keep the code and assets self-contained within the file."

Prompt Template: Data Extraction

One-liner:
> "Extract all YouTube links from this HTML."

Expanded version:
> "You will receive a block of raw HTML containing embedded iframes from various media sources. Write a JavaScript function that can be run in the browser console to extract and list only the source URLs from YouTube and SoundCloud embeds. Output the results as a clean array of URLs. Ignore any malformed or duplicate entries."

The shift from one-liner to structured prompt doesn't mean adding fluff—it means adding purpose. You're helping the model visualize what "done" looks like. The difference in results is usually dramatic: tighter code, cleaner logic, more usable interfaces, and fewer follow-up edits.

But you don't have to start big. Many of the most effective prompts begin as rough ideas and grow through prompt layering—where you build up features or constraints one at a time.

For example:

1. "Build a basic flight sim in 3D."
2. "Add realistic camera movement and speed controls."
3. "Include fog for depth and a shimmering ground texture."
4. "Prevent the user from flying off the edge of the map."

Each step adds clarity and complexity. Gemini handles this layering well—retaining context as you refine.

The other trick is knowing when to use tools like ChatGPT to assist with prompt crafting. You can take your vague idea and say:

> "Turn this into a more detailed prompt for Gemini to generate a visual 3D app."

It's like having a prompt coach on hand—translating messy ambition into something models can digest.

In the end, prompting is less about being perfect from the start, and more about learning how to talk to the model like a collaborator. Start with the idea. Expand the ask. Tighten the scope. Clarify the result.

And suddenly, your prompts stop being requests—and start becoming blueprints for real things.

From Querying to Co-Thinking: Getting It Right More Often

When people get a bad response from an AI, the blame often goes straight to the model. "It's hallucinating." "It got confused." But more often than not, the issue traces back to something subtler: how the question was framed—or worse, how much was left unsaid.

Prompting isn't foolproof, even with a model as powerful as Gemini 2.5 Pro. The biggest mistakes users make tend to fall into a few predictable buckets. The good news? They're easy to spot—and fix—once you know what to watch for.

Common Mistake #1: Vague Instructions

Let's say you prompt:
> "Write code for a calculator."

Sounds fine. But what kind of calculator? Command line or GUI? What language? Basic arithmetic or scientific functions?

When the model guesses, you've already lost control.

To fix this, anchor your prompts with clear scope and format. Even adding two extra details—like "Python with a GUI using Tkinter, supports add/subtract"—can dramatically improve the output. Models are powerful, but they're not mind readers. Specificity unlocks precision.

Common Mistake #2: Asking for Too Much at Once

People often stack a dozen tasks into a single prompt.
> "Build a blog, integrate a newsletter, add user auth, connect to a CMS, and style it like Apple."

That's not a prompt. That's a roadmap.

The result? Gemini will either ignore half of it, hallucinate pieces, or spit out scaffolding that doesn't really do anything well.

Instead, break it up. Start with the foundation. Then build iteratively—just like you would with a human collaborator. Ask for step one, then move forward with context preserved. Think in layers, not lists.

Common Mistake #3: Trusting Unverified Output

Even when Gemini nails the tone, format, or structure, the output might still contain errors. A coding snippet might reference a non-existent function. A fact might be outdated. An instruction might sound plausible—but be wrong.

This isn't a dealbreaker. It's part of the territory. Just like working with a junior dev or researcher, you verify before you ship.

When you're dealing with code or factual info, always ask follow-up questions like:

- "Is this method still supported in the latest version?"
- "What's the source for this claim?"
- "Can you re-check this logic?"

It doesn't slow you down. It makes you smarter about the loop.

Shifting from Prompting to Co-Thinking

The biggest mindset shift is realizing that you're not just throwing questions over a wall. You're in a dialogue. The model doesn't just respond—it adjusts. Learns from your corrections. Builds on what you're trying to do.

When you prompt Gemini with the attitude of "generate this," the interaction ends quickly. But if you prompt with "here's what I'm trying to explore—what's the best way to approach it?" you open the door to co-thinking. Now the model isn't just a tool. It's a partner in reasoning.

For example, instead of:

> "Write a script that visualizes a neural net."

Try:

> "I'm trying to help students visualize how neurons activate in a basic neural net. What's a simple way to animate this in JavaScript? Can you walk me through the steps before generating code?"

You'll get a more thoughtful answer. And the next prompt will be more collaborative by nature.

It's a small shift. But over time, it changes how you use AI.

You're not just asking for outputs anymore. You're asking for strategy, structure, and shared insight.

You're not just driving. You're navigating together.

And that's when things start to click—not because you're prompting harder, but because you're prompting smarter.

At first glance, prompting seems simple. But under the surface, it's a kind of dialogue—part programming, part persuasion, part design. The best results don't come from giving more instructions. They come from giving the right ones, at the right time, with the right mental model of how your AI partner "thinks."

Gemini 2.5 Pro is powerful. But like any tool, its value expands when you understand how to shape it. Prompting isn't just a technical trick. It's a creative discipline—one that turns you from a user into a co-creator.

Learn to prompt well, and you're not just using AI more effectively.

You're learning to think with it.

CHAPTER 9

THE COMPETITIVE LANDSCAPE AND WHAT' S COMING NEXT

Every breakthrough invites a race. As Gemini 2.5 Pro reshapes what's possible with AI, the rest of the field is adapting—fast. OpenAI, Anthropic, Meta, Deepseek, and XAI are all pushing forward, each with their own strengths, architectures, and philosophies. But it's not just about who has the smartest model anymore. It's about who can scale, ship, integrate, and evolve—all at once.

This chapter looks at the current players, their positions, and what their trajectories say about where AI is heading next. Because Gemini may be leading now—but this race is far from over.

Challengers Rising: Vision, Precision, and the Push to Keep Up

Gemini 2.5 Pro may have taken the spotlight, but in the background, other players haven't stopped moving. In fact, some are making quietly impressive strides—especially OpenAI and Deepseek. While their approaches differ, both are chasing the same thing: relevance in a new landscape where Google now sets the pace.

OpenAI, the early king of the hill, recently rolled out a suite of updates under its GPT-4.0 umbrella—particularly on the visual side. While Gemini brought shock with its multimodal performance, OpenAI responded with a serious push into multi-turn image generation. Instead of producing a single static image from a one-shot prompt, GPT-4.0 now supports iterative refinement: you describe a character, it sketches it; you say "make it darker, add fog, give them a cape," and it updates accordingly. This opens the door to dynamic creativity, especially for designers, marketers, and game creators who want fast iteration with visual control.

It also rolled out better diagram interpretation, making GPT-4.0 stronger at handling symbols, structured visuals, and layouts embedded with data. Whether it's a Venn diagram, a floor plan, or a basic wireframe, the model doesn't just see the image—it understands the relationships within it. This capability isn't flashy, but it's deeply valuable for technical fields: STEM education, architectural planning, UX research.

While OpenAI focuses on polishing depth and refinement, Deepseek has gone all-in on raw speed, open access, and affordability.

Initially seen as an underdog, Deepseek's open-source models drew attention for how far they pushed within tight compute budgets. But their real leap came with the release of Deepseek V3—a distilled model that, despite running lean, performs competitively on many reasoning and coding benchmarks.

What stands out with Deepseek V3 isn't just its performance—it's how it runs. Paired with Groq's custom inference hardware, V3 generates answers blazingly fast, often outperforming GPT-3.5 or Claude 2 in latency-heavy tasks. Developers who care more about throughput than subtlety are flocking to it. And in use cases like real-time querying, chatbot infrastructure, or embedded AI in products, speed matters as much as intelligence.

Deepseek's rise also signals a broader trend: AI is decentralizing. Not everyone wants to rely on closed APIs. V3 and future open checkpoints could empower startups and independent devs to self-host powerful models without paying OpenAI or Google prices.

Still, neither OpenAI nor Deepseek is sitting comfortably. Both are facing pressure—from users, from expectations, and from Gemini's massive context window and low latency. The gap has narrowed—but also sharpened.

This new wave of competition isn't about who can generate the prettiest response.

It's about who can scale intelligence, access, and control at once—and who can do it next.

When Momentum Doesn't Translate: Grok, Meta, and Apple on the Sidelines

For all the energy in the AI space, not every big name is thriving. Some are stalling. Others are simply missing the moment. And despite early hype, a few are starting to show just how hard it is to turn vision into working infrastructure.

Let's start with Grok, the flagship model from Elon Musk's XAI.

When Grok launched, it came with the usual Musk-style fanfare: witty tone, internet-native branding, baked into X (formerly Twitter), and marketed as the open, uncensored alternative to "woke AI." For a while, that angle drove curiosity—and some adoption. But when it came to actual performance? The cracks started showing quickly.

Despite promises of advanced reasoning and web-native behavior, Grok's outputs have been inconsistent at best. Real-world comparisons show it lagging behind GPT-4, Claude, and Gemini in coherence, reasoning depth, and especially in coding. Most notably, there's still no public API, which makes it almost impossible for developers to build real products around it. For all of Musk's ambition, Grok remains trapped inside X—more of a novelty than a tool.

Even more telling: the XAI team's silence on benchmarks. Unlike OpenAI, Google, or Anthropic, which actively publish test results and invite comparison, Grok's creators tend to stay vague, leaving users to piece together its strengths from a handful of tweets. In a space where transparency matters, that alone raises red flags.

Then there's Meta—the original AI heavyweight that somehow missed the moment.

Meta has talent. It has research. It has the open-source LLaMA family. But it lacks one thing: execution.

While Meta's models are solid on paper, the company seems disconnected from the actual developer workflows shaping AI's future. Their tooling is slow to adopt. Their API offerings are limited. And they continue to treat AI like an R&D project—not like the product platform it's becoming. LLaMA 2 and 3 have made some progress, especially among the open-source crowd. But they're not leading. They're reacting.

As for Apple, its absence speaks volumes.

Apple's AI silence isn't just a product strategy—it's a structural flaw. The company has spent years championing on-device privacy and minimal data collection, which is great for trust—but terrible for training. As a result, Apple lacks the datasets needed to train competitive frontier models, and it hasn't shown serious public investment in large-scale LLM infrastructure. Siri, once promising, has become a meme for what voice assistants can't do.

And while Apple does have cutting-edge hardware—M chips that are fast and efficient—it hasn't bridged that into a real AI platform. Developers can't train or run large models natively. There's no Apple-hosted API. No developer-facing LLM ecosystem. Just whispers of something coming "in the next iOS update."

In an AI race that's moving at warp speed, Apple is jogging quietly in the wrong lane.

What unites all three of these players—XAI, Meta, and Apple—is the same root issue: misalignment between vision and infrastructure.

They have the names. They even have the capital. But they don't have the full-stack strategy that companies like Google are executing on. They're not building around developers, creators, or products. They're chasing headlines or over-indexing on internal research.

And in this phase of the AI race, that's no longer enough.

What wins now isn't just intelligence.

It's intelligence that ships, scales, and sticks.

Silicon Wars and the Shape of What's Coming

Beneath the benchmarks and prompting strategies, another battle is unfolding—one that has less to do with language and more to do with silicon. Because as these models grow smarter and more demanding, raw performance isn't enough. The future will be decided not just by who has the best model—but by who can run it fastest, cheaper, and at scale.

That's why we're now seeing the rise of a custom hardware arms race—and the stakes are enormous.

Companies like Groq, Cerebras, NVIDIA, and Google are each fighting for dominance at the infrastructure layer, building chips and systems purpose-built for large model inference and training. But while their goals align, their approaches couldn't be more different.

Groq has taken a radical route—offering inference speeds so fast, you can barely watch the token generation happen. Paired with lean models like Deepseek V3, Groq's chips chew through prompts at unreal speeds, sometimes 10x faster than mainstream GPU stacks. It's not as flexible as NVIDIA's toolkit, but for specific tasks—like real-time chat, agents, or low-latency applications—Groq's single-minded speed is disruptive.

Cerebras, meanwhile, is thinking big. Literally. Their wafer-scale chips dwarf anything on the market, designed to handle entire model architectures without splitting across multiple GPUs. Ideal for training large models with massive context, Cerebras is betting on vertical integration at the hardware level, where everything from memory to processing sits on one gigantic slab of silicon.

But none of them can be ignored like NVIDIA—the undisputed giant, still dominating general-purpose training and inference. While others innovate, NVIDIA continues to set the pace with its GPU ecosystem, CUDA tooling, and near-monopoly on the compute used by OpenAI, Anthropic, and many others. The shift may be coming—but as of now, most of the AI world still runs on NVIDIA's terms.

And then there's Google—the only player building both the model and the chips under the same roof. Its TPUs are tailor-made for Gemini. That gives Google total control over optimization, power efficiency, and deployment, enabling things like the million-token context window and nearly cost-free latency inside AI Studio. Unlike NVIDIA's more universal approach, Google's hardware is deeply specific—and that's exactly what gives them the edge.

It's no longer just about model size.

It's about the marriage between model and machine.

And over the next 6–12 months, that hardware advantage will directly shape the AI breakthroughs we see next. Here's where the momentum is pointing:

- Context windows will double (or more). Google has already teased 2 million tokens. Others will follow—unlocking whole-codebase reasoning, video transcript recall, and novel use cases in law, research, and storytelling.

- Multi-agent orchestration will go mainstream. We'll stop thinking in single prompts. Instead, you'll see frameworks where AI "teams" collaborate—planner agents, code agents, search agents—all working on one outcome. Gemini, GPT-4, and Claude are already heading this way.

- Real-time AI agents will start replacing traditional tools. Need to build a website? Instead of browsing templates or installing plugins, you'll talk to an agent that generates it, edits it, and deploys it live. Design, coding, research, testing—AI won't just assist. It will own workflows, moment to moment.

- Hardware-optimized models will become the default. Like Apple designs chips around software, AI labs will build models explicitly for the hardware they run on. Gemini already does this. Others will follow—because that's the only way to maintain performance while scaling up.

- The line between product and platform will blur. AI will stop being something you use once in a while. It will be ambient, integrated, and persistent—baked into tools, conversations, and workflows. It won't just answer your questions. It will remember your intent.

The question is no longer whether AI will change how we work, think, and create.

It's who will deliver it first—and how far they can take it.

The race is wide open.

But the infrastructure is being built now.

The AI landscape is crowded, ambitious, and volatile—but that's exactly what makes it powerful. Each lab brings something unique: OpenAI with its research velocity, Anthropic with its alignment-first approach, Deepseek with open models, and Google with full-stack domination. What we're seeing isn't just competition. It's convergence—a future where models aren't just smarter, but more useful, embedded, and personalized.

Gemini 2.5 Pro lit a spark. What comes next is the fire it started—across labs, across platforms, across every part of how we work, learn, and build.

CHAPTER 10

THE COST OF CREATION: ECONOMICS OF SCALE IN AI

For all the talk of intelligence, benchmarks, and creativity, there's a quieter force driving the AI revolution: economics. Behind every prompt, every model run, and every new tool is a cost—tokens in, tokens out, infrastructure humming in the background. And the further AI reaches, the more those costs start to matter—not just for companies, but for creators, teams, and everyday users.

This chapter unpacks what it really costs to run a model like Gemini 2.5 Pro at scale, why Google is able to do it cheaper than nearly anyone else, and how pricing models, rate limits, and infrastructure choices are shaping the future of who gets to build with AI—and who gets left behind.

Cheap, Fast, Powerful: How Google Shifted the Price Curve

The power of an AI model used to be tied to how much you could afford to spend. Better performance meant higher cost. Longer context windows meant ballooning bills. For years, this was the accepted tradeoff—especially when models like GPT-4 entered the scene. They were strong, but expensive to scale.

Then came Gemini.

More specifically, Gemini Flash—Google's lightweight model optimized for speed and cost-efficiency. And it didn't just shift expectations. It broke the economic model entirely.

Real-world usage numbers tell the story better than any spec sheet. One developer running a high-volume AI platform shared a shocking stat: over 1 million messages processed through Gemini Flash cost just $1,200 total.

Compare that to Claude 3, OpenAI's GPT-4-turbo, or even 3.5-tier models, and the difference is massive.

In that same usage report:
- Claude 3.5 Sonnet (comparable reasoning quality): ~$31,000 for the same message volume.

- GPT-4 Turbo: more efficient than the original GPT-4, but still considerably higher than Gemini.
- Even GPT-3.5, while "cheaper," cost over 5x more than Gemini Flash at scale.

That's not a margin. That's a massive moat.

And yet, performance didn't suffer. In many creative and coding workflows, Gemini Flash produced results comparable to GPT-4 or Claude 3.7—faster, and at a fraction of the cost.

This cost structure isn't just a pricing strategy. It's the result of total vertical integration.

Google isn't paying for someone else's cloud. It runs Gemini on its own custom TPUs, through its own cloud infrastructure, backed by years of product optimization. That means it can control latency, throughput, and token costs in a way no other provider—except maybe Groq or Cerebras—can currently match.

And that's exactly why Google is playing a different game.

While competitors try to balance model intelligence with infrastructure costs, Google's figured out how to run smarter models cheaper—and offer them to developers with fewer limits, faster response times, and generous context windows.

It's not just about making AI more accessible.

It's about reshaping the cost structure of innovation.

And the more Gemini improves, the harder it becomes for others to justify charging 10–20x more for similar results.

The Claude Cost Problem—and Google's Structural Advantage

Numbers don't lie, and in this case, they're hard to ignore. In a high-volume real-world deployment, Claude—Anthropic's flagship model—racked up a usage cost of $31,000 for less than half the message volume processed by Gemini Flash for just $1,200.

That's not just expensive. It's economically unsustainable for most builders.

Claude's models are undeniably sharp. They perform well on reasoning, comprehension, and context retention. But they come with a price tag that puts pressure on scaling, especially in production environments. For startups running LLM-powered features, that cost gap can mean the difference between launching a product—or shelving it entirely.

So how does Google offer similar or better performance, at more than 25x lower cost?

It comes down to the most underappreciated formula in AI:

Hardware + Cloud + Science = Economic Edge.

Let's unpack that.

Hardware: Google doesn't rely on NVIDIA GPUs or third-party compute vendors. It runs Gemini on its own Tensor Processing Units (TPUs)—hardware specifically engineered for AI workloads. These chips are optimized not for broad compatibility, but for Gemini itself. That makes them cheaper to operate, faster at inference, and more energy-efficient at scale.

Cloud: Unlike OpenAI (dependent on Microsoft Azure) or Anthropic (running on AWS), Google owns the full stack—Google Cloud Platform (GCP). This gives them control over infrastructure, routing, deployment, and scaling. It also means no middleman costs, and better integration across AI Studio, Vertex AI, and beyond.

Science: Behind Gemini is a legacy of research leadership. From inventing the transformer architecture to leading in multimodal modeling, Google Research doesn't just build what's next—it optimizes it from the start. Gemini is trained with efficiency in mind, allowing it to perform at high quality with fewer wasted parameters and tighter alignment between task and output.

When these three forces combine, the result is a model that doesn't just work well—it works cheaply, reliably, and at scale.

This is where competitors get stuck.

OpenAI builds great models, but it rents infrastructure. Anthropic produces safe, aligned systems, but relies on expensive GPU stacks and third-party cloud platforms. Deepseek offers speed, but lacks the tight integration of chip-to-cloud. Even Groq, for all its raw speed, doesn't own a model—only the silicon.

Only Google currently holds all three pieces: the model, the chips, and the global cloud.

That means Gemini isn't just a tool—it's the tip of a larger system optimized for one thing: scalable intelligence that doesn't break the budget.

And that's not just a technical win. It's a business one.

Because in AI, the real cost isn't how smart your model is—it's what it takes to run it for the next million users.

Who Gets to Build: Cost, Access, and the AI Economy Ahead

It's easy to look at AI cost comparisons and think of them as back-end concerns—issues for enterprise buyers, cloud architects, or procurement teams. But in reality, the economics of AI are shaping who gets to create, and who gets locked out before they even start.

For startups, cost is existential. Building a product that leans on large language models isn't just about performance—it's about whether the business can sustain the API bill while it finds product-market fit. If one model costs 25x more to run than another with comparable output, it's not a toss-up. It's a dealbreaker.

This is why Gemini—especially the Flash tier—is gaining traction with lean teams. It offers reliability, creative capability, and fast iteration without forcing founders to burn runway on token costs. You can build smarter prototypes, test with users faster, and scale without taking on infrastructure debt too early. For a generation of AI-first startups, that cost curve is now a strategic advantage.

Developers—freelancers, hobbyists, indie hackers—face a different challenge: they're not worried about million-token prompts or agentic orchestration (yet). They want tools that respond quickly, generate usable code, help with debugging, or produce assets on the fly. But even they bump into rate limits, usage caps, and per-token charges.

Gemini's freemium model via AI Studio gives them breathing room. It means they can experiment, learn, and build without constantly watching the meter. That freedom fuels momentum—and momentum is what gets projects off the ground.

Then there's the education space, where the impact of cost is arguably even greater.

Teachers, students, and instructional designers aren't operating with enterprise budgets. They're often hacking together tools, running AI experiments in the classroom, or creating custom learning experiences for underserved groups. For them, even a modest usage cost can be a barrier. But Gemini's cost-efficiency—especially when building flashcards, lesson plans, or simulations—makes it far more accessible than Claude or GPT in the current landscape.

In short: when AI gets cheaper, more people get to create. More kids build their first game. More teachers customize lessons. More startups survive the early phase. And more developers push boundaries not because they're funded, but because they're free to try.

Still, this raises important questions about the future.

How long can this cost advantage last?

Will models like Gemini Flash always be free—or is a pricing shift inevitable?

We're already seeing hints. Google has positioned Gemini 2.5 Pro as experimental, with higher rate limits—but has also acknowledged that monetization is coming soon. Vertex AI pricing tiers are in development. API access will be metered. What we're living through now may be a moment of strategic generosity, not a permanent reality.

That leads us into the next phase of the AI economy: freemium modeling at scale.

Just like cloud storage, productivity software, or developer tools before it, AI is likely headed toward usage tiers, credits, premium features, and paywalls. The trick will be balancing openness for creators with sustainability for platforms.

Who gets the best models? Who gets access to long context? What features stay free—and which get gated?

These aren't just business decisions.

They're decisions that shape who gets to imagine, build, and learn in the next wave of the internet.

For now, Google has thrown the gates open—and the builders are pouring in.

But as monetization tightens, the real test will be who can keep the doors open wide enough to spark the next generation of creators—without putting a price tag on the creative process itself.

The future of AI won't be determined by IQ alone. It will be shaped by access—who can afford to build, who can scale their ideas, and who can run powerful models without breaking the bank. Right now, Google has cracked the code: speed, performance, and scale at an unprecedented cost advantage.

But that edge won't last forever.

As more labs race to close the gap—and open-source models grow more competitive—the economics of AI will become the next frontier of innovation. Not just faster models, but smarter systems—that run leaner, adapt better, and deliver value without excess.

Because in the age of creation, it's not just what you build that matters.

It's what it costs to make it real.

CHAPTER II

WHAT THIS MEANS FOR YOU

After all the benchmarks, models, breakthroughs, and demos, the biggest question left is the most personal: What does this mean for you?

Whether you're a builder, a teacher, a founder, a learner—or just someone trying to keep up—Gemini 2.5 Pro and models like it aren't just shaping the future of technology. They're reshaping how people think, work, and create today. This chapter isn't about what the model can do. It's about what you can do now that this model exists.

If You're a Developer: The Playground Just Doubled in Size

If you write code, this isn't just a technical upgrade—it's a paradigm shift. Gemini 2.5 Pro didn't just become a better model. It became a new kind of development environment, one that speaks your language, handles your scale, and gets out of your way.

Whether you're building solo or part of a team, the immediate opportunities are real.

Start with vibe coding—small, self-contained projects where the fun is the point. These are perfect for exploring Gemini's reasoning, speed, and creative coding ability. Snake games, Lego builders, visualizations in Three.js or Pygame, even weird toys like surgery sims or particle explosions—these aren't gimmicks. They're rapid feedback loops. And they're where you'll start to feel the model's strengths without being buried in scaffolding.

Then move up to agent-style workflows: tools that plan, reason, generate, and test in one loop. Gemini excels here because of its token window and internal "thinking" phase. You can walk it through logic, context, exceptions, and edge cases. Ask it to reason before coding. Ask it to sketch before scaffolding. It doesn't just output code—it collaborates on approach.

Explore SweetBench-style tasks—code transformation, refactoring, editing, converting functions between languages. Gemini 2.5 Pro outperforms earlier versions and many peers here. For legacy cleanup, documentation generation, or API wrapper creation, it's shockingly effective with minimal prompting.

Also: lean into long context workflows. If your codebase is big—really big—Gemini's 1M token window (and the coming 2M expansion) is your unlock. Feed in files, describe your goals, and let it map the pieces. Some devs are already using it for full-repo analysis, automatic docstring generation, and onboarding support. This isn't coming. It's happening now.

But manage your expectations, too.

Gemini is powerful, but it's not perfect in editors. If you use tools like Cursor or VS Code with LLM integration, the "thinking" models can still get tangled, overplan, or hallucinate under pressure. Sometimes, simpler models respond faster and cleaner for basic completions. This means part of your workflow now involves choosing the right model for the right task—not just defaulting to the biggest brain in the room.

And don't ignore the ecosystem shift.

With Google integrating Gemini deeper into GCP, Firebase, and DevTools, you're going to see AI baked into everything from testing frameworks to deployment pipelines. Learning how to prompt for infrastructure, not just code, is going to be part of the next developer skillset.

The bottom line?

Gemini isn't just another model to benchmark.

It's a co-developer. One that's always on, speaks full-stack, and costs less than a coffee break. And the sooner you treat it like a teammate—not just a tool—the faster you'll build what you've been waiting to try.

Here's the next section of Chapter 11, written directly to business leaders and decision-makers—focused, strategic, and grounded in what Gemini 2.5 Pro means for operations, innovation, and competitive positioning:

If You're a Business Leader: The Cost of Waiting Just Got Higher

If you're leading a company, managing a team, or shaping product strategy, Gemini 2.5 Pro should have your full attention—not just for what it can do, but for what it signals: the speed of innovation has outpaced traditional planning cycles.

This is no longer about "exploring AI someday." The businesses adapting now will build leaner, iterate faster, and unlock capabilities others won't even realize are possible until it's too late.

So where do you start?

First, assess your core workflows: customer service, content creation, internal tooling, R&D, analytics, onboarding, documentation, QA. Anywhere you're currently paying for human labor to follow repeatable patterns—Gemini can likely prototype an alternative in days, not quarters.

Use Gemini Flash or 2.5 Pro in experimentation sprints. Assign small teams to explore how prompts can replace legacy processes. Don't wait for enterprise integrations—go directly to AI Studio and test on real tasks. The latency is low, the cost is negligible, and the learning curve is short.

If you're investing in product development, start looking at AI not just as a feature—but as a layer. Ask: how can your product become AI-native? What would it look like if Gemini could reason over a user's entire interaction history, generate tailored flows, or build user-facing tools on demand? Think about agentic behavior—not just answers, but actions taken in context.

You'll also want to pay attention to talent workflows. Early-stage teams are using Gemini to reduce onboarding time, create technical documentation, generate training materials, and even write performance feedback summaries. If you're still treating LLMs as novelty assistants, you're missing the managerial leverage they now provide.

From an infrastructure angle, Gemini's cost profile shifts the financial model. Compare the Gemini Flash deployment that processed 1 million messages for $1,200 to Claude's $31,000 for half the volume. That's not a discount. That's a strategic moat for any business that builds on top of it.

Finally, prepare for internal resistance. AI adoption is not always a technical problem—it's cultural. Teams worry about job displacement, quality control, or losing creative identity. Address this head-on. Make AI augmentation part of upskilling, not outsourcing. Show your teams how to think with AI, not fear it.

The winners in this next phase won't just be the most technically advanced.

They'll be the ones who move first, build with intent, and learn faster than their competitors.

Gemini makes that possible.

Now it's your move.

If You're a Learner: Build First, Understand Faster

This is your moment. If you're trying to learn—coding, design, business, writing, science—AI isn't just a tool for answers anymore. With Gemini 2.5 Pro, it's a learning environment, a personal tutor, a project partner, and a feedback engine all in one.

The old way was slow: watch tutorials, try to follow along, get stuck, search forums, maybe give up. Now? You write a prompt like "Teach me how to build a weather app in HTML and JavaScript with comments in every section," and it hands you a working example instantly—annotated, runnable, and ready to tinker with.

The fastest learners today aren't memorizing more. They're building earlier. Gemini makes that possible.

Want to learn Python? Don't read about syntax for a week. Prompt Gemini to create five mini projects that teach core concepts: variables, loops, conditionals, and functions. Ask it to explain the logic in plain English. Ask follow-ups until it clicks.

Learning biology? Use Gemini to simulate cell behavior or visualize immune responses. Studying math? Ask it to walk you through a step-by-step solution, then challenge it to quiz you with increasing difficulty.

And if you're preparing for exams—SATs, MCATs, GMATs, AIME, whatever—Gemini doesn't just regurgitate answers. It can create custom practice problems, explain concepts with analogies, generate flashcards, and act as an interactive whiteboard tutor, adjusting to your level and pace.

You don't need to wait for the "right" materials anymore. You create them as you go.

The best part? You're not limited to your subject. Want to learn how to build a game, animate a character, scrape data, or write a business plan? Gemini doesn't care what field you're in. It adapts. And if your prompt is vague, it helps you refine it—until you're not just learning, you're thinking like a builder.

This is what Education 2.0 really means. Not just AI answering your questions, but helping you ask better ones. Learning becomes a loop: try → break → fix → understand → level up. Faster, deeper, and way more hands-on than traditional formats.

Here's your edge: don't just consume.

Create to learn.

Use Gemini to write, build, break, and explore. It's not about perfect prompts. It's about getting your hands dirty, adjusting along the way, and letting curiosity lead.

You don't need to wait for a class or a course or a credential.

You just need a prompt—and the courage to try.

If You're Just Curious: Start Simple, Stay Curious

You don't need to know code. You don't need a technical background. You don't need a plan. If you're here with nothing but curiosity, that's more than enough—because Gemini 2.5 Pro is built to meet you where you are.

This isn't about jumping into complex prompts or building full apps overnight. It starts with one question. One experiment. One spark.

Try this:
> "Explain how a Rubik's Cube works in simple terms."
> "Help me create a fun short story set in space."
> "I want to build a website, but I've never coded. Where do I start?"

You'll be surprised how it responds—not just with answers, but with conversation. It's designed to work with you, not at you. If something's confusing, ask it to explain it another way. If the answer doesn't feel right, question it. Gemini doesn't get frustrated. It adjusts.

That's the real magic—not in what the model knows, but in how it helps you learn what you care about.

Start small. Give it a recipe to remix. Ask it to turn your messy notes into a poem. Use it to plan a trip. Write a letter. Learn a new skill at your own pace. The barrier to entry is lower than it's ever been—not because you've caught up to AI, but because AI now reaches out to meet you.

This isn't about keeping up with the experts. It's about unlocking what you can do—what you've wanted to try, create, build, or explore, but didn't know how. Gemini doesn't replace your creativity. It gives it momentum.

And here's the truth: no one has it all figured out. Not the devs. Not the executives. Not even the researchers.

Everyone is learning. Everyone is experimenting.

The difference is that some people start, while others wait until it feels safe.

So don't wait.

You don't need permission. You just need curiosity.

And a model that's finally ready to think with you.

The tools are here. The barriers are down. The excuses are gone.

You don't need a team. You don't need a degree. You don't need permission. With the right prompt and a clear vision, you can build apps, visualize data, simulate systems, teach, learn, and explore at a scale that was science fiction just months ago.

Gemini 2.5 Pro changed the game. But the real story isn't the model.

It's what people will do with it next.

And that includes you.

CONCLUSION – THINK. PROMPT. BUILD.

REPEAT.

We started with a moment—when Gemini 2.5 Pro hit the scene and shifted the tempo of the entire AI race. Not with noise, but with capability. Not with theory, but with proof. From solving puzzles and building web apps to simulating life systems and rewriting the rules of coding, it showed us what happens when intelligence, speed, and scale converge.

But this book hasn't just been about Gemini.

It's been about what this kind of model means for the world around it—and the people inside that world. Developers now have a co-creator that writes, reasons, and adapts. Businesses have infrastructure that's cheaper, faster, and more flexible than ever before. Educators have a learning tool that's interactive, personalized, and always-on. And learners—curious, messy, wildly ambitious—have a playground that rewards questions over credentials.

Here's the truth: AI is no longer just software. It's a creative engine. A thinking partner. A tool for invention, education, exploration, and expression. It can write with you. Build with you. Explain, simulate, imagine. It can even argue, refine, and surprise. Used well, it extends the mind—not replaces it.

But here's the catch: powerful tools come with responsibility. This isn't the time to use AI blindly. It's the time to use it thoughtfully. That means understanding what these models are good at—and what they're not. It means questioning outputs, checking assumptions, and staying aware of how AI shapes attention, behavior, and power. Because we're not just users in this new era.

We're participants.

And that means our prompts matter. Our choices matter. Our creativity matters.

So don't just watch this moment pass by.

Start with one idea. One tool. One experiment.
Think with it. Prompt it. Build something. Break something. Learn. Then do it again.

This is how you stay ahead.
This is how you stay informed.
This is how you stay in it.

The world is changing fast. But the frontier is open.

And it belongs to the ones who are willing to step forward and create.

APPENDICES

Appendix A: Glossary of Terms

A quick-reference guide for readers who want to understand core AI concepts without technical overload:

Token
A unit of text used by language models to process input and generate output. A word like "build" is one token; "building" might be two. Most models calculate cost and capacity based on tokens, not characters.

Context Window
The amount of information (measured in tokens) a model can process at once. Gemini 2.5 Pro supports up to 1 million tokens—an industry-leading window—allowing it to handle full codebases, long documents, and complex simulations.

Inference
The process of running a model to generate an output from input. When you prompt an AI, you're triggering an inference process. Faster inference means quicker responses.

TPU (Tensor Processing Unit)
Google's custom AI hardware designed to train and run models like Gemini efficiently. Unlike traditional GPUs, TPUs are tightly integrated with Google's infrastructure, offering superior speed and cost control.

Multimodal
A model that can process and generate across different media types: text, images, audio, code, and more. Gemini 2.5 Pro is natively multimodal.

Grounding
Connecting AI responses to real-world data or search results to improve accuracy. Gemini supports grounding through Google Search when enabled.

One-shot Prompting
A prompt that generates a complete, complex output in a single interaction—no back-and-forth needed.

Thinking Models
Models like Gemini 2.5 Pro that simulate an internal reasoning phase before producing output, improving logic and problem-solving.

Appendix B: Prompt Library

Use these curated one-shot prompts to experiment with Gemini's capabilities.

Games
- "Create a Python snake game using Pygame with glowing trail effects, power-ups, and speed modifiers."
- "Build a 3D Lego brick simulation using Three.js with snapping mechanics, camera controls, and rotation."

Web Apps
- "Write a single-file HTML/CSS/JS to-do list app with dark mode toggle and task priority filters."
- "Generate a full-stack blog in one file with markdown support, local storage, and responsive styling."

Education
- "Simulate a virus attacking cells using HTML and JavaScript with interactive sliders for replication rate and white blood cell defense."
- "Generate flashcards from this biology textbook excerpt, formatted for Anki import."

Simulations
- "Create a 3D torus knot visualization in Three.js with GUI controls for color, speed, and shape."
- "Build a toy surgery simulator with click-to-cut mechanics, scoring system, and health tracker."

Use these prompts as-is or evolve them into expanded versions with roles, constraints, or output format requests for even better results.

Appendix C: Benchmark Reference Charts

LMSYS Chatbot Arena (March 2025)
- #1 Gemini 2.5 Pro
  - ELO: 1443
    - Beats GPT-4.5, Claude 3.7 Sonnet, Groq-3, and Deepseek V3

PolyMarket (Feb 2025 Spike)
- Gemini win odds jumped from 12.6% → 94% overnight
- Groq fell from 83.5% → 4%
- Largest reversal in platform history

SweetBench (Agentic Code Performance)
- Gemini 2.5 Pro: 63.8%, custom agent setup
- Significantly higher than Gemini 2.0, competitive with Claude 3

AIME & GPQA Benchmarks (Math & Science)
- AIME 2025: 86.7%
- GPQA (Science): 84%

These charts reflect Gemini's leadership in reasoning, coding, and long-context tasks.

Appendix D: Model Comparison Table

Feature	Gemini 2.5 Pro	GPT-4. 5 Turbo	Claude 3.7 Sonnet	Deepseek V3
Context Window	1M tokens (2M soon)	128K tokens	200K tokens	128K tokens
Speed (latency)	Very fast	Moderate	Moderate-slow	Extremely fast (Groq)
Multimodal	Yes (native)	Yes (text → image)	Yes (limited)	Text + code only
Coding Performance	High (agentic code)	High (stable code)	High reasoning	Strong for devs
One-Shot Capabilities	Excellent	Good	Inconsistent	Good (needs tuning)
Pricing	Very low (Flash:	High	Expensive	Low (open weights)

	$1,200/1M msgs)		(Claude: $31K/50oK msgs)	
Hardware Dependency	TPUs (Google-owned)	Azure (OpenAI/Microsoft)	AWS (Claude)	Groq/NVIDIA
API Maturity	Studio + Vertex AI	Mature	Mature	In progress

ABOUT THE AUTHOR

Zaida T. Huffman is a future-focused writer, researcher, and creative technologist exploring the intersection of intelligence, design, and human potential. With a passion for making complex systems approachable, Zaida translates emerging technologies into clear, compelling narratives that empower builders, thinkers, and curious minds.

Driven by the belief that AI should expand access—not gatekeep it—Zaida's work combines sharp analysis with hands-on insight, giving readers both the "why it matters" and the "what to do next." Her writing bridges the gap between innovation and impact, demystifying cutting-edge tools without dumbing them down.

Think. Prompt. Build. is more than a title—it's Zaida's personal mantra. Whether she's writing books, teaching workshops, or collaborating on AI-powered projects, her mission remains the same: help people understand the world that's coming, and give them the tools to shape it.

When she's not writing, Zaida can be found deep in a build session, obsessing over prompt structures, or teaching others how to work alongside machines—with creativity, curiosity, and control.